Fresh Dialogue Nine / New Voices in Graphic Design

In/Visible: Graphic Data Revealed

"I think of reporting as the source of every visualization.... Visualizations are interesting only because they reveal something about an interesting set of data, an interesting piece of information."

—STEVE DUENES

"I'm not really concerned with accuracy. Of course, it's important to fall back on accurate data, but what interests me most is the storytelling."

—ANDREW KUO

"When we think about visualizations as a way to communicate, it really changes the design implications and the possibilities of bars, charts, and diagrams."

—FERNANDA VIÉGAS

Fresh Dialogue Nine / New Voices in Graphic Design

In/Visible: Graphic Data Revealed

With a foreword by Emma Presler

Princeton Architectural Press
American Institute of Graphic Arts New York Chapter
New York, 2009

Published by
Princeton Architectural Press
37 East Seventh Street
New York, New York 10003

For a free catalog of books, call 1.800.722.6657.
Visit our website at www.papress.com.

AIGA/NY
164 Fifth Avenue
New York, New York 10010
www.aiga.org

Mission
EXCLUSIVE/INCLUSIVE
DEBATE/DISCUSS
YOU/US
BUSINESS/COMMUNITY
RANTS/RAVES
PROFITABLE/SUSTAINABLE

ART/COMMERCE
DOGMATIC/PRAGMATIC

US/YOU

THE MISSION OF AIGA/NY
IS TO IDENTIFY AND DEFINE ISSUES
CRITICAL TO ITS MEMBERSHIP
AND THE GRAPHIC DESIGN PROFESSION;
TO EXPLORE AND CLARIFY THESE ISSUES
FOR THE PURPOSE OF HELPING TO ELEVATE
THE STANDARDS OF THE BUSINESS
OF GRAPHIC DESIGN;
AND TO CREATE A FORUM FOR THE
EXCHANGE OF INFORMATION, VIEWS,
IDEAS, AND TECHNIQUES AMONG THOSE
ENGAGED IN THE PROFESSION.

Printed and bound in China
12 11 10 09 4 3 2 1 First edition

Fresh Dialogue Chair: Emma Presler
Fresh Dialogue Committee Member: Liz Danzico
Fresh Dialogue Committee Member: Laura Forde

Editor: Nicola Bednarek
Designer: Paul Wagner
Fresh Dialogue Series Design: Jan Haux and Deb Wood

Special thanks to: Nettie Aljian, Sara Bader, Janet Behning, Becca Casbon, Carina Cha, Penny (Yuen Pik) Chu, Russell Fernandez, Pete Fitzpatrick, Wendy Fuller, Jan Haux, Clare Jacobson, Aileen Kwun, Nancy Eklund Later, Linda Lee, Laurie Manfra, John Myers, Katharine Myers, Lauren Nelson Packard, Jennifer Thompson, Joseph Weston, and Deb Wood of Princeton Architectural Press —Kevin C. Lippert, publisher

Library of Congress Cataloging-in-Publication data is available from the publisher.

Contributors

Steve Duenes

Andrew Kuo

Fernanda Viégas

—

Moderator

John Maeda

—

Date

23 May 2008

—

Location

The TimesCenter, New York

Contents

Foreword by Emma Presler

Fresh Dialogue Chair 2008; board member and secretary, AIGA/NY 2006-2008

The AIGA/NY's annual Fresh Dialogue series introduces new talent and concepts to the design community. Over the past twenty-four years, the event has evolved into a unique forum that is equal parts visual showcase and idea incubator, offering insights into the prescient work of designers. The decision to document these events in book form underscores the recognition that the series has become a bellwether for the design industry, capturing the collective zeitgeist at its most formative stage.

Information graphics—this year's theme—do much the same thing. Charts, graphs, diagrams, and maps capture information in midstream, visualizing concepts and data in static and dynamic formats. They provide instant perspective, situating issues in metaviews that make connections and patterns self-evident. This sense-making service has made information design ubiquitous and, paradoxically, its practitioners largely invisible.

In this election year, recognizing the influential place information design and its makers occupy seemed timely and overdue. Charts, graphs, diagrams, and maps shape popular perceptions of candidates and constituencies in print, online, and broadcast mediums, at times superseding the influence of political pundits. Additionally, interesting questions of ethics, judicious simplicity and seductive complexity, interpretive storytelling, and accurate reporting all come into play in visual journalism.

Information designers are not supposed to express an explicit point of view on the content they visualize. That authorship distinction is too frequently bestowed on the editor, writer, statistician, or analyst who provides the data, leaving the designer cast in the role of executor. This transference of editorial authority, however, diminishes the design choices that affect the interpretation of the data. In fact, it is the numerous design decisions on color, line, format, orientation, font, and much more that make the content embedded in charts, graphs, diagrams, and maps accessible. In this expanded role, the information designer becomes editorial arbiter, wielding equal influence.

Board colleagues and Fresh Dialogue committee members Laura Forde and Liz Danzico played crucial roles in the choice of participants and in helping shape the scope of this topic. Steve Duenes, Andrew Kuo, and Fernanda Viégas lent unparalleled expertise, grace, and wit to the proceedings. John Maeda's guidance elevated the evening to something akin to an art happening. I extend my thanks and gratitude to each of them for a successful investigation of graphic data revealed.

Background conversation

. . .

Enter Emma Presler

EMMA PRESLER: Good evening, everyone, and welcome to Fresh Dialogue. Fresh Dialogue has been a tradition at AIGA/NY since the chapter started, for more than twenty-four years now. In the early days, it served as a forum to showcase fresh design talent, but over the last two years we've tried to expand the notion of "fresh" to include new and emerging ideas in design—new topics and new approaches. While information graphics aren't particularly new, its practitioners are, at least to a degree. The designers behind all of the charts and graphs you see every day in various media have so far remained relatively anonymous. We felt it was time to shine a spotlight on information graphics as a design discipline and on the designers who create them—especially during an election year when we're all inundated every day with more graphs and charts than we can possibly take in.

Applause

When we presented this idea to the AIGA in New York, we encountered a bit of skepticism. People were concerned that the topic was a tad cerebral, a little bit nerdy. Well, I'm happy to say that we sold this event out today, which kind of proves that hypothesis wrong. And as one of our panelists once said, I guess the dork vortex is a large vortex.

Laughs

So tonight, panelists Steve Duenes, Andrew Kuo, and Fernanda Viégas are going to talk about issues such as the ethics behind effective data, simplicity versus complexity, the differences between objective and subjective data, and the role that humor can play in charting accessible routes through data.

It's my pleasure to introduce John Maeda, who'll guide us through this discussion. Maeda has become known worldwide for his inventive merging of technology and art. He brings his hybrid skills as a graphic designer, artist, and computer scientist to his new role as the sixteenth president of the Rhode Island School of Design (RISD). He is the recipient of numerous awards, including the National Design Award, and has work in the permanent collection of the Museum of

Modern Art. His most recent book, *The Laws of Simplicity*, has been published in fourteen languages and has become the hallmark text for advocates of simplicity in the digital realm. He's clearly overqualified for the role of moderator, and we're thrilled to have him with us. Please join me now in giving him a warm welcome.

Applause

* * *

Enter John Maeda

JOHN MAEDA: Thank you, nerdy people. It's exciting that you have all come here tonight to see fresh people. I was once fresh myself—I actually participated in a Fresh Dialogue about ten or twelve years ago. And now that I've become unfresh, I'm happy to present the fresh. But before I introduce tonight's panelists, I wanted to get you all in the mood by talking a bit about what I've been occupied with for the last few years. As you will see, I've been a bit confused. I stumble through things, looking for something new like a squirrel looking for shiny things.

Laughs

It all started with my curiosity about the computer, which, to me, has always been a weird device. When I was a teenager, I had a computer called the Apple II. Did anyone have an Apple II? Oh, nerd quotient is high. This is the most I've ever seen.

Looks around as some people in the audience raise their hands

Many of you remember the Apple II as a device that you'd be very excited to buy—it cost around $1,800—you'd bring it home, plug it in, turn it on, and then—it would do absolutely nothing at all. Do you remember

Laughter

[1]

]10 PRINT "MAEDA"
]20 GOTO 10
]

that? It just blinked at you, like a very fancy lamp. There was no software out there. There was no Microsoft or instant messaging or network. You would be lucky if you had a printer. It was a time when all you could do was program, so I'm showing you here the first program I created. [1] We all know this program: It's a kind of vanity program, where the computer would print your name over and over again. Forever. A great program—very uplifting if you're depressed like me.

Laughs

In this era they also published books that were called *Instant Activities for Your Apple*, *Growing Up with Computers*, and the like, with a free poster in each copy. [2] [3] These were great books because they were very simple. Today, you can buy books on how to program Java in twenty-four days or how to program PHP in seventeen days, but they turn out to be very long and complicated, not exactly a twenty-four-day project. If they made PHP books like those old Apple books today, we could all program on PHP. Simple books are the kind of books that we need out there right now. And that reminds me of the simpler times in my own life.

Laughs

When I was a child, I had this moment when I realized that I was good at art and math, but my parents, who are your typical blue-collar immigrant family, would always say, "John is really good at math." Period. When I went to MIT, however, I was able to defect a bit. I discovered the book *Thoughts on Design* by the great Paul Rand, and it changed my whole life.

Laughs

[2]

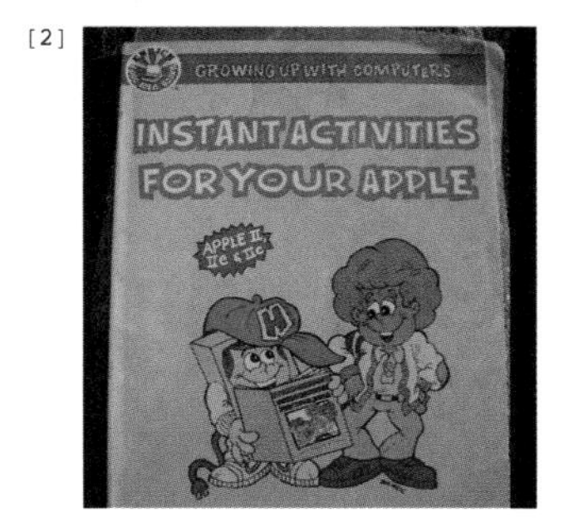

[3]

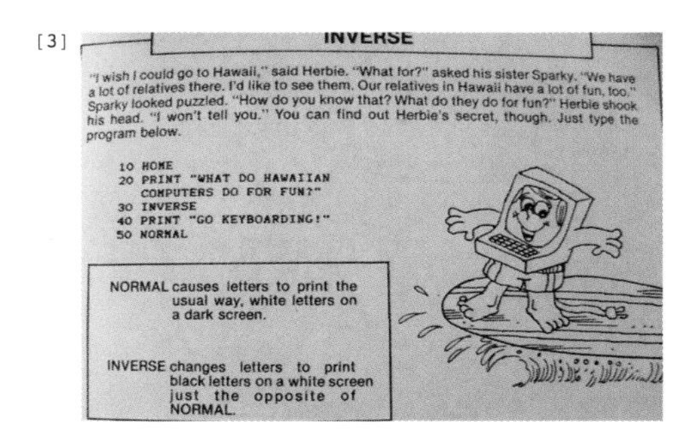

INVERSE

"I wish I could go to Hawaii," said Herbie. "What for?" asked his sister Sparky. "We have a lot of relatives there. I'd like to see them. Our relatives in Hawaii have a lot of fun, too." Sparky looked puzzled. "How do you know that? What do they do for fun?" Herbie shook his head. "I won't tell you." You can find out Herbie's secret, though. Just type the program below.

```
10 HOME
20 PRINT "WHAT DO HAWAIIAN
   COMPUTERS DO FOR FUN?"
30 INVERSE
40 PRINT "GO KEYBOARDING!"
50 NORMAL
```

NORMAL causes letters to print the usual way, white letters on a dark screen.

INVERSE changes letters to print black letters on a white screen just the opposite of NORMAL.

[4][5][6] He really impressed me with his insightful visual vocabulary, thoughtful writing, humor, and childlike appreciation for the visual domain. Reading his book made me realize that I wanted to do something like this, this design thing. So because of him I switched careers. I finished my masters at MIT, I went to art school, I reprogrammed my brain.

I also left the computer. At MIT I had e-mail as early as the 1980s. At art school I suddenly had no computer—it was like heaven. Rand, in one of his books, mentions a Yale student who said, "I came here to learn how to design, not how to use the computer." Design schools, take heed. This was in the late 1980s when there was a lot of controversy between the computer people and noncomputer people. So for a while, I really enjoyed my computerless life.

Then people died and time passed, and eventually, I began to come back to the computer. I became less crusty, and I began to play with the computer. In the early 1990s, I made a program that looks a lot like Adobe Illustrator and was called Illustrandom. [7] It has just one feature: If you select a point on the curve, you can play with a dial and the curve begins to move. I'll never forget my graphic design teacher, who saw the program and said, "This is really great, John, but can you make it stop now?" But it doesn't stop. You're using the computer, so you don't have to make it stop, you can go on forever. The computer's a strange device, it is freest in this form of always changing.

Laughs

[4]

[5]

Around that time I did an experiment in Japan that involved people drawing without their hands. I would have someone sitting down drawing a picture using four human pens, a black pen, red pen, blue pen, and a green pen. They were named Mr. Black, Mr. Red, Mr. Blue, and Mr. Green, and each of them held the corresponding color of pen in their hand. The goal was to draw by simply telling Mr. X what to draw without the use of gestures, sketches, and so forth. It was a great challenge because it's hard to draw without your hands. It's like super art direction. Participants would say, "Draw from the right to the middle," but it was hard to get good at this. The concept is similar to using a computer, because it enables you to draw with a thousand pens, a million pens. So the experiment was really about simulating how to use a computer. One of the participants figured out how to use an X/Y axis, and suddenly his hands were free. He could say, "Draw from X2 to Y5." Ironically, he drew the most boring picture. It was a house that looked like a CAD drawing.

Laughs

So what does that tell us? It tells us that when you constrain the way you draw to the way a computer works, you end up drawing like a computer would. It was an interesting insight at the time.

Also around this time I began to wonder what happens when you create things on a computer that last forever; for example, when you make a form that continuously changes based on movements along an X or Y axis, what is that form? The movement is a way to

[6]

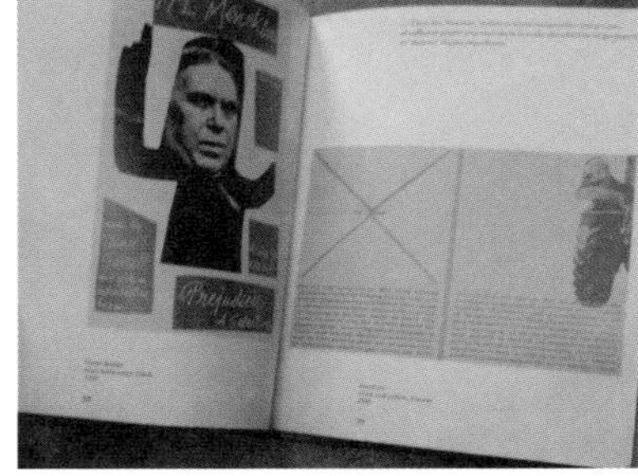

[7]

The user-interface of "illustrandom" mimics the bezier editing interface common to many illustration packages

unwrap the form into multiple dimensions. The computer has no dimensional limitations, so you can see a kind of four-, five-, or six-dimensional visual.

While I was amazed at the possibilities of the computer, I also began to be stressed out by the computer world. For example, I had to finish a project, and there was this one pixel that I wanted to erase. You probably remember when Photoshop introduced layers and it got hard. So the question was, which layer is that pixel on? I'll never forget how I searched every layer for the pixel that I wanted to erase. In the end it turned out that it was a piece of dust on the screen.

Laughter

These kinds of anomalies kept happening in my life, and it started to bother me, because they affected how I thought. So around 2000, I began to focus less on the computer and instead started to make objects. I made paintings in which I embedded palm pilots. [8] I made LED sculptures as an attempt to create a simpler computer [9], and I began to make objects out of MDF (medium-density-fiberboard). [10] This lamp is made out of a bento box, it's a rice lamp. [11] In London last year, I sculpted objects out of iPods, for example this iPod fish. [12] [13]

Laughs

Besides making things, I'm also interested in found objects, because I think that the world is like one big museum. I'll never forget how hard it was for me to understand the concept of the circle/triangle/square. The circle is a strong shape, but it is kind

[8]

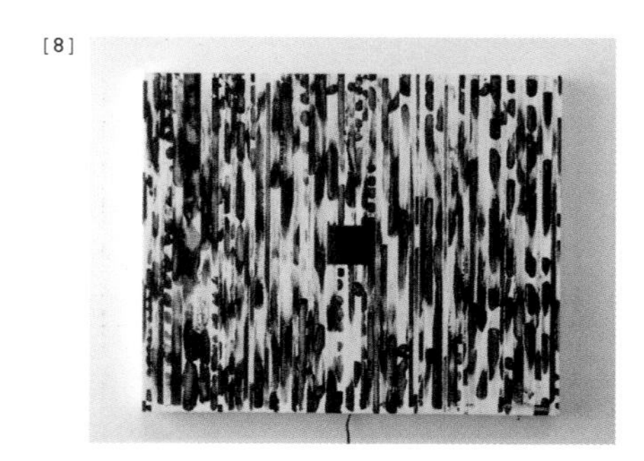

[9]

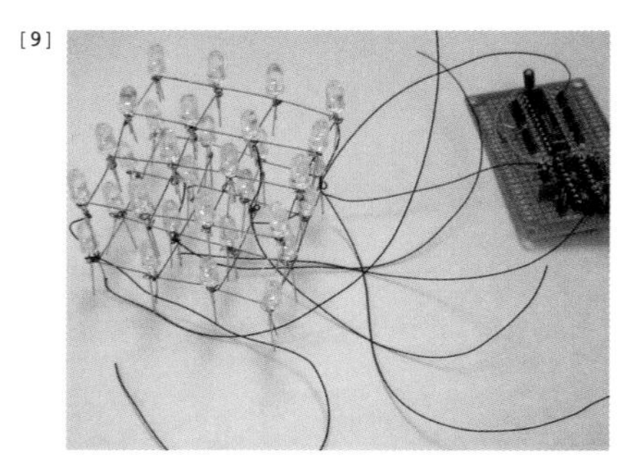

[10]

[11]

[12]

[13]

of unstable. It's plain and simple. The triangle I've always thought of as the punk rocker shape. It's unstable, but it's cool. The square is boring, but you can count on it. [14] And the world is full of these shapes: When I'm on the beach, I'll always look for the circle/triangle/square. Last year on Cape Cod, I saw them everywhere. [15] It's intoxicating to see the world talking to you in our vocabulary of circle/ triangle/square.

Another found object that caught my attention was this phone at London, Heathrow. [16] It must be the simplest phone to use: There's no button, you can only call one number. When I returned to Heathrow this year, I saw that the phone's technology had been updated: Now it's a touch-tone one-button phone. [17] It's a digital upgrade.

Laughs

In 2003, I began to think about simplicity and complexity. I didn't like how simplicity is often just a covering around what sits as complex [18], and so I thought what if it looked like this instead? [19] What if it was a sort of gray expanse where complexity and simplicity naturally coexisted, what would that feel like? [20]

I also began to see signs; for example, when I looked at the word *simplicity*, I found the letters MIT in it. [21] [22] In both words, *simplicity* and *complexity*, I found MIT. [23] [24] I was wondering whether I should take that as a sign to stay at MIT. I basically had a career crisis because this sign said, "Don't do

Laughs

[14]

[15]

[16]

[17]

[18]

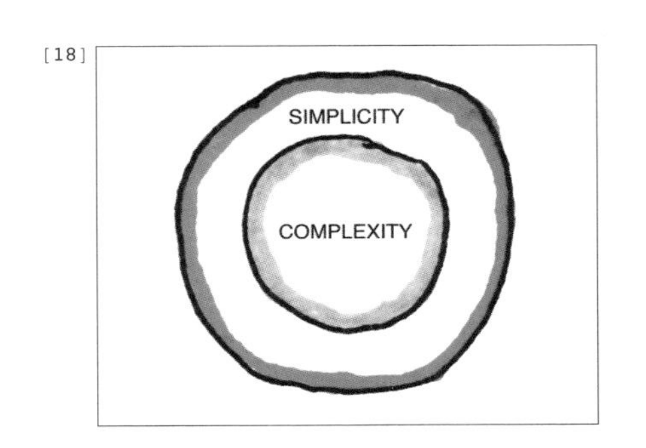
SIMPLICITY
COMPLEXITY

[19]

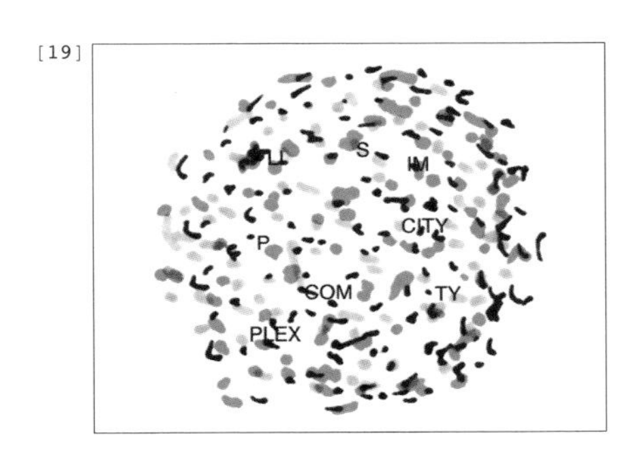
S
IM
CITY
P
COM
TY
PLEX

[20]

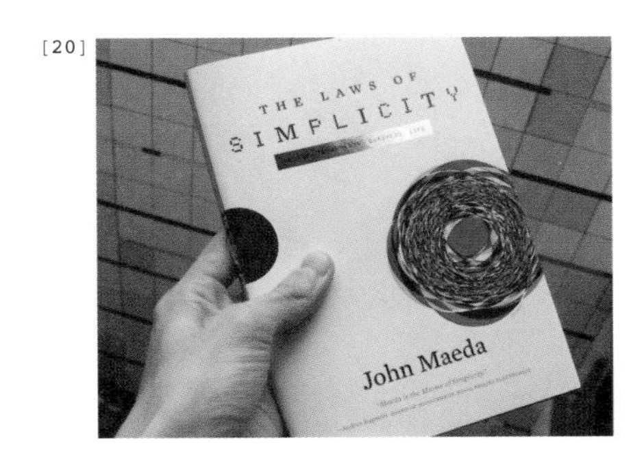
THE LAWS OF
SIMPLICITY
John Maeda

[21]

[22]

[23]

[24]

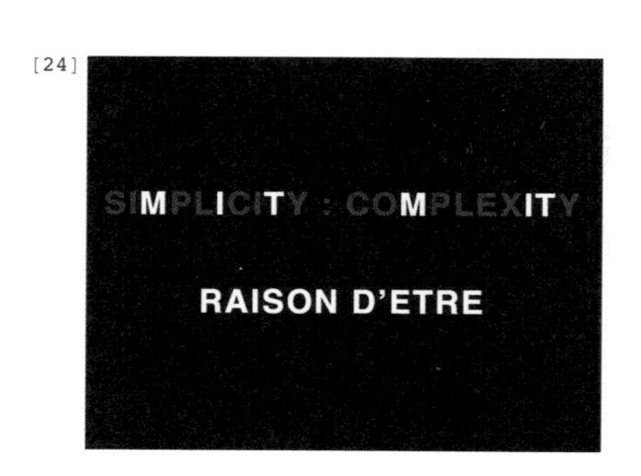

[25]

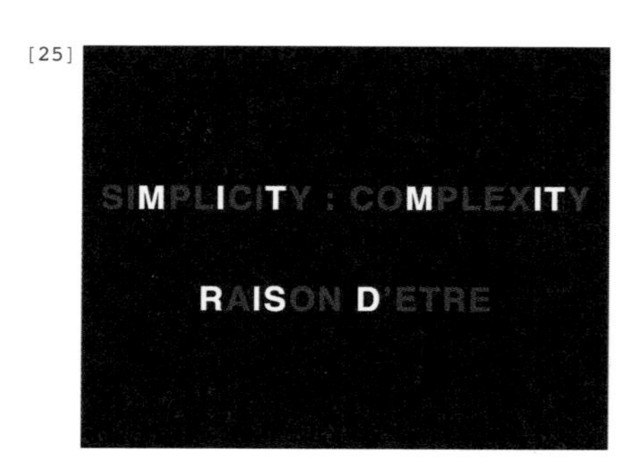

[26]

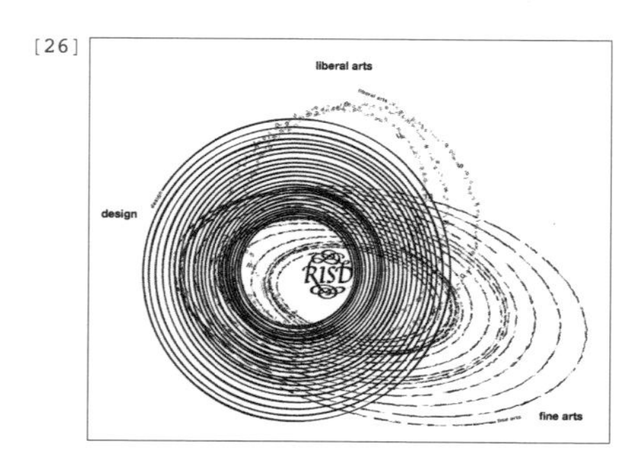

anything but MIT." But then I came across the French word *raison d'etre*, which is also a very important word. And I discovered that there's R-I-S-D in there [25], so that new sign allowed me to move to the next step of my life and to become the new president of RISD. [26]

Laughs

But I think it's time now to introduce tonight's panelists, because Fresh Dialogue is about fresh people, and I'm not fresh anymore. I'm excited to present three fresh, fresh people. First of all, we have fresh Steve Duenes, who oversees the graphics department of the *New York Times*. Then we have Andrew Kuo, who looks a bit like my little brother and who is an artist and RISD graduate. His work addresses fears and anxieties in charts and other forms. And the third fresh speaker is Dr. Fernanda Viégas of IBM. I'm sure you've seen her work on the Web. So let's begin with the fresh voices. Steve, come on up!

Laughs

Applause

Enter
Steve Duenes

DUENES: Thank you. As John mentioned, I lead the graphics department at the *New York Times*, which is mostly responsible for the charts and maps and diagrams that appear in the newspaper and on the *Times*'s website. Often when I tell people what I do, they ask if my group is the group that does the pie charts. And sadly, yes, we are the group that does the pie charts. [27] And we do the bar charts . [28] But we also do more complicated figures than that, and I want to show you some of our work tonight.

Laughs

In this case [29], for example, my colleague Amanda Cox was looking at volatility in the stock market. Toward the end of 2007, the stock market experienced a fair amount of volatility, so she decided to place that in context. In her chart, each of the vertical gray bars represents a daily swing in percentage change for the Dow. As the figure shows, there really was a bit of volatility recently, but it was nothing compared to what we saw during the late 1920s and early 1930s.

[27] "Exit Polls," *New York Times*, 2008, designer: Archie Tse [28] "Military Spending," *New York Times*, 2005, designer: Hugh K. Truslow [29] "Measuring Volatility," *New York Times*, 2008, designer: Amanda Cox

[27]

Believes the most important issue in this race is ...

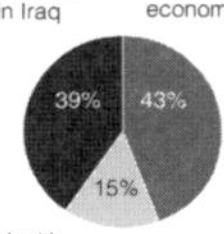

make a decision about whom they would support, with about one-third saying they did not decide whom to vote for until the final week of the campaign. Although Mrs. Clinton had held a lead for months, Mr. Obama appeared to get a significant bounce after receiving the backing of the state's senior senator, Edward M. Kennedy. One local poll this week showed Mr. Obama slightly edging ahead of Mrs. Clinton. The state's 93 pledged delegates are allocated proportionally between the two candidates, with 31 based on the statewide results and the remainder divided based on the

Believes the most important issue in this race is ...

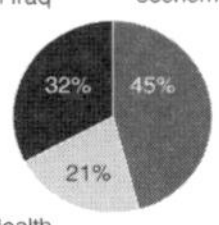

The economy was cited as the top issue by a large swath of voters, which divided evenly between the two candidates. But voters who identified Iraq as the top issue sided with Mr. Obama two to one. While Mrs. Clinton had shown a significant lead in several statewide polls, Mr. Obama had collected more money from the state than any other candidate, raising $2 million. Mrs. Clinton had the backing of several top Connecticut Democrats, including Richard Blumenthal, the state's attorney general and a former classmate of Mrs. Clinton's at the Yale Law School. In recent days, Mr.

Believes the most important issue in this race is ...

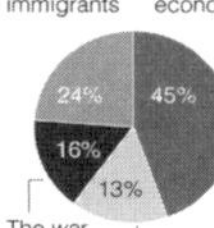

George W. Bush by nearly tw
Romney dismissed the 11th h
Cain, saying, "I've got a lot of
Many observers had said that

[28]

RIC SCHMITT

ON, Feb. 7 — The Pen-
t of $419.3 billion for
year increases spend-
illion, or 4.8 percent,
evels even as it calls
aircraft carrier and
l number of the new-
ombat jet.
ding proposals offered
ush on Monday, which
by personnel and op-
contain no money to
ons in 2006 in Iraq and
which have been aver-
billion a month.
costs of military and
efforts in Iraq and Af-
ugh the end of 2005,
ation in coming days
pplemental budget, ex-
the range of $81 bil-
another supplemental
start of next year, ad-
nd Pentagon officials

llion of the anticipated
request for this year
military activities,
Army, which provides
rces in Iraq and Af-
Army would receive

Military Spending

The military budget proposed Monday does not include money for operations in Iraq and Afghanistan, which have been financed by supplemental appropriations in the past few years.

Supplemental appropriations

$500 billion
400
300
200
100

'80 '85 '90 '95 '00 '05 '10

Estimated

Estimated supplemental military appropriations for 2005 have not yet

amphibious trans
toral combat shi
ammunition ship
for retiring an ai
ming the carrier
The Air Force
combat jet, the F
receive $4.3 billio
the money would
production cappe
about 100 fewe
planned. A larger
proposed for the J
a new combat je
Air Force, Marine
Anticipating a s
cisions to close o

Around $8
may be sou
operations
Afghanista

bases in the Unit
seas, the budget

[29]

SOAPBOX

MEASURING VOLATILITY

Daily changes in the **Dow Jones industrial average**

The dark lines show the **daily fluctuations** in the index.

The color shows how the index performed in a **year**.

DECREASE | INCREASE
-25 -10 0 +10 +25%

DAILY CHANGE
+10%
+5
-5
-10

1907 bank panic
1929 crash
President Dwight D. Eisenhower has a heart attack
Inflation rises; bond prices become more volatile
Black Monday
Russia defaults
Sept. 11, 2001

1900s 1910s 1920s 1930s 1940s 1950s 1960s 1970s 1980s 1990s 2000s

Overall volatility — and economic uncertainty — peak during the Great Depression

Market reopens after closing during part of World War I

Nasdaq composite

In its early years, the Nasdaq was often used as a proxy for the movement of smaller stocks. But it became dominated by technology stocks, and its volatility accelerated in the late 1990s.

+10%
+5
-5
-10
Index peaks in March 2000

The Pulse of Uncertainty

GRAPHIC ESSAY

There is no question that volatility on Wall Street increased last year, and many analysts expect the rockiness to continue in 2008.

But 2007 may have seemed especially tumultuous only because the years before it were remarkably calm. There was only one day from 2004 to 2006 when the Dow Jones industrial average moved up or down by more than 2 percent. Last year, amid concerns about the subprime mortgage sector and credit markets in general, swings that large occurred 14 times.

Historically, though, 14 times is not exceptional: that total ranks about average over the last 10 years and slightly less than that over the last 20. The Standard & Poor's volatility index, or VIX, which measures expectations of future volatility based on the prices of options, also ended the year near its 10-year average.

Taken another way, if the Dow's daily changes — the dark lines in the chart — were stacked end to end, they would stretch about 110 percentage points from July to December of last year. That compares with nearly 200 percentage points in the second half of 2002, when the market was shaken by corporate scandals.

In 2007, some of the most volatile stocks in the S.&P. 500 were **E*Trade Financial**, **Countrywide Financial** and **MBIA**, a company that specializes in guaranteeing the financial health of others.

Among stocks that gained value, **MEMC Electronic Materials,** whose silicon wafers are used by semiconductor and solar cell producers, and **Amazon.com** had the most drastic swings.

"Internationally and domestically, there are things that are a little unsettling," said G. William Schwert, a finance professor at the University of Rochester. "But in the scope of things, it's not that unusual."

Mr. Schwert has studied why volatility changes over time. His answers include bank panics, wars and recessions.

AMANDA COX

Shanghai composite

Last February, an investing scare in China sent markets tumbling around the world. But it was only a temporary setback — one of several last year. Shares in Shanghai fell by at least 1.5 percent once a week, on average, but they still ended the year up nearly 100 percent.

+10%
+5
-5
-10
Feb. 27

Source: Bloomberg THE NEW YORK TIMES

One of the things we try to do in the graphics department is to respond to news with interesting forms and to develop graphics that illuminate the data that we report. The next chart [30] illustrates the Terri Schiavo case of 2005. There was a court battle between Schiavo's husband and her parents over whether or not her feeding tube should be removed. We gathered a lot of information about the case moving up and down in the courts, from the local Florida courts all the way up to the U.S. Supreme Court and back down. We started to talk about the data, to think about a pattern that might exist within it, and discovered that it felt a lot like a fever line chart, something that just moves up and down. So we're not afraid to riff off of familiar forms and to transfer them to new topics when we're covering a story.

We also try to develop very simple forms when we deal with stories that come up regularly. When we covered the Supreme Court rulings of 2002 and 2003, we came up with a simple way of conveying a lot of information visually by altering the saturation level on a series of photographs. [31] We didn't invent this concept; we borrowed it from someone who did it for something else, but it worked well.

[30] "A Winding Legal Road," *New York Times*, 2005, designer: Matthew Ericson
[31] "Major Rulings of the 2002-2003 Term," *New York Times*, 2003, design: Staff

[30]

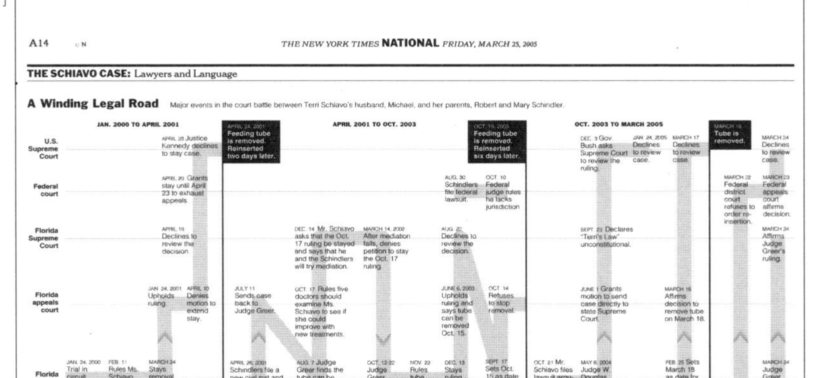

A14 N THE NEW YORK TIMES **NATIONAL** *FRIDAY, MARCH 25, 2005*

THE SCHIAVO CASE: Lawyers and Language

A Winding Legal Road

Major events in the court battle between Terri Schiavo's husband, Michael, and her parents, Robert and Mary Schindler.

JAN. 2000 TO APRIL 2001

U.S. Supreme Court
APRIL 23 Justice Kennedy declines to stay case.

Federal court
APRIL 20 Grants stay until April 23 to exhaust appeals.

Florida Supreme Court
APRIL 18 Declines to review the decision.

Florida appeals court
JAN. 24, 2001 Upholds ruling.
APRIL 10 Denies motion to extend stay.

Florida court
JAN. 24, 2000 Trial in circuit court: Judge George W. Greer presides.
FEB. 11 Rules Ms. Schiavo would have chosen to have tube removed.
MARCH 24 Stays removal until after appeals are exhausted.

APRIL 24, 2001 Feeding tube is removed. Reinserted two days later.

APRIL 2001 TO OCT. 2003

Federal court
AUG. 30 Schindlers file federal lawsuit.
OCT. 10 Federal judge rules he lacks jurisdiction

Florida Supreme Court
DEC. 14 Mr. Schiavo asks that the Oct. 17 ruling be stayed and says that he and the Schindlers will try mediation.
MARCH 14, 2002 After mediation fails, denies petition to stay the Oct. 17 ruling.
AUG. 22 Declines to review the decision.

Florida appeals court
JULY 11 Sends case back to Judge Greer.
OCT. 17 Rules five doctors should examine Ms. Schiavo to see if she could improve with new treatments.
JUNE 6, 2003 Upholds ruling and says tube can be removed Oct. 15.
OCT. 14 Refuses to stop removal.

Florida court
APRIL 26, 2001 Schindlers file a new civil suit and motion to introduce new evidence in the closed case. **Judge Frank Quesada orders tube reinserted.**
AUG. 7 Judge Greer finds the tube can be removed. Later in the month, he delays removal to allow for appeals.
OCT. 12-22 Judge Greer holds hearing on new medical treatments.
NOV. 22 Rules tube should be removed Jan. 3.
DEC. 13 Stays ruling pending appeals.
SEPT. 17 Sets Oct. 15 as date for removal.

OCT. 15, 2003 Feeding tube is removed. Reinserted six days later.

OCT. 2003 TO MARCH 2005

U.S. Supreme Court
DEC. 3 Gov. Bush asks Supreme Court to review the ruling.
JAN. 24, 2005 Declines to review case.
MARCH 17 Declines to review case.

Florida Supreme Court
SEPT. 23 Declares "Terri's Law" unconstitutional.

Florida appeals court
JUNE 1 Grants motion to send case directly to state Supreme Court.
MARCH 16 Affirms decision to remove tube on March 18.

Florida court
OCT. 21 Mr. Schiavo files lawsuit arguing new law is unconstitutional.
MAY 6, 2004 Judge W. Douglas Baird rules law is unconstitutional.
FEB. 25 Sets March 18 as date for removal of feeding tube.

Laws passed
OCT. 21, 2003 Florida Legislature passes "Terri's Law"; **Gov. Jeb Bush orders tube reinserted.**

MARCH 18 Tube is removed.

U.S. Supreme Court
MARCH 24 Declines to review case.

Federal court
MARCH 22 Federal district court refuses to order re-insertion.
MARCH 23 Federal appeals court affirms decision.

Florida Supreme Court
MARCH 24 Affirms Judge Greer's ruling.

Florida court
MARCH 24 Judge Greer rules state agency can't intervene.

Laws passed
MARCH 21 U.S. Congress passes bill allowing federal lawsuit.

Sources: Kathy L. Cerminara, Shepard Broad Law Center, Nova Southeastern University; Kenneth W. Goodman, University of Miami Ethics Programs

Matthew Ericson/The New York Times

[31]

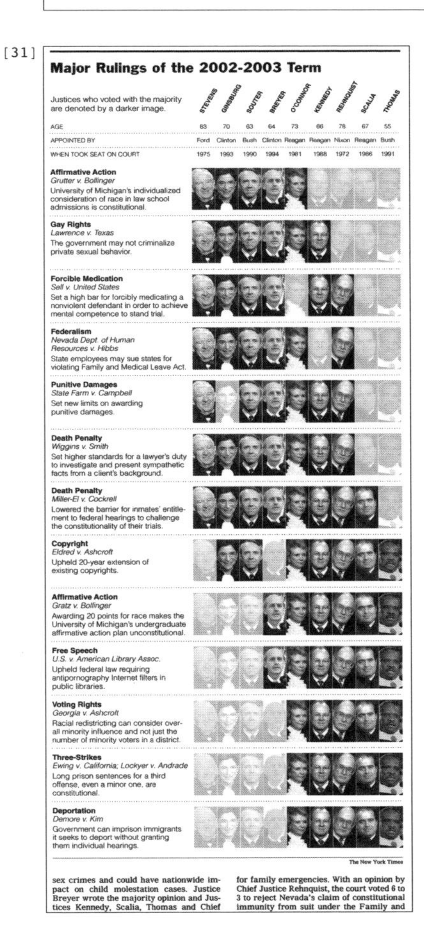

Major Rulings of the 2002-2003 Term

Justices who voted with the majority are denoted by a darker image.

	STEVENS	GINSBURG	SOUTER	BREYER	O'CONNOR	KENNEDY	REHNQUIST	SCALIA	THOMAS
AGE	83	70	63	64	73	66	78	67	55
APPOINTED BY	Ford	Clinton	Bush	Clinton	Reagan	Reagan	Nixon	Reagan	Bush
WHEN TOOK SEAT ON COURT	1975	1993	1990	1994	1981	1988	1972	1986	1991

Affirmative Action
Grutter v. Bollinger
University of Michigan's individualized consideration of race in law school admissions is constitutional.

Gay Rights
Lawrence v. Texas
The government may not criminalize private sexual behavior.

Forcible Medication
Sell v. United States
Set a high bar for forcibly medicating a nonviolent defendant in order to achieve mental competence to stand trial.

Federalism
Nevada Dept. of Human Resources v. Hibbs
State employees may sue states for violating Family and Medical Leave Act.

Punitive Damages
State Farm v. Campbell
Set new limits on awarding punitive damages.

Death Penalty
Wiggins v. Smith
Set higher standards for a lawyer's duty to investigate and present sympathetic facts from a client's background.

Death Penalty
Miller-El v. Cockrell
Lowered the barrier for inmates' entitlement to federal hearings to challenge the constitutionality of their trials.

Copyright
Eldred v. Ashcroft
Upheld 20-year extension of existing copyrights.

Affirmative Action
Gratz v. Bollinger
Awarding 20 points for race makes the University of Michigan's undergraduate affirmative action plan unconstitutional.

Free Speech
U.S. v. American Library Assoc.
Upheld federal law requiring antipornography Internet filters in public libraries.

Voting Rights
Georgia v. Ashcroft
Racial redistricting can consider overall minority influence and not just the number of minority voters in a district.

Three-Strikes
Ewing v. California; Lockyer v. Andrade
Long prison sentences for a third offense, even a minor one, are constitutional.

Deportation
Demore v. Kim
Government can imprison immigrants it seeks to deport without granting them individual hearings.

The New York Times

sex crimes and could have nationwide impact on child molestation cases. Justice Breyer wrote the majority opinion and Justices Kennedy, Scalia, Thomas and Chief

for family emergencies. With an opinion by Chief Justice Rehnquist, the court voted 6 to 3 to reject Nevada's claim of constitutional immunity from suit under the Family and

During the 2004 political conventions we struggled to come up with a graphic that conveys something interesting. It's hard to know exactly what to cover during the conventions, as they're canned events. We started to talk about the speeches that were given, the words that were used, and decided to chart them in a way that emphasized the themes the parties were expressing. We borrowed the visual form—essentially, a tag cloud—from a chart that *Fortune* magazine had published in the 1940s. It turned out to be really interesting: When you look at the chart [32], you see that the use of the word *war* is similar in frequency for the Democrats and the Republicans, whereas the use of the word *health care* shows quite a bit of difference. The pattern exposed the contrast between the two parties and the themes they were trying to get across.

We also looked at the patterns that existed for individual speakers. As you can see, Republican speakers stressed national security themes, while Democrats looked at domestic issues. Then we borrowed from our own form to create a chart that we've used for a few years now to look at President Bush's State of the Union addresses. [33] The word frequencies in his speeches really convey his emphasis on different themes at different times.

[32] "The Words Speakers Use," *New York Times*, 2004, designer: Matthew Ericson [33] "The Words That Were Used," *New York Times*, 2006, designer: Matthew Ericson

[32]

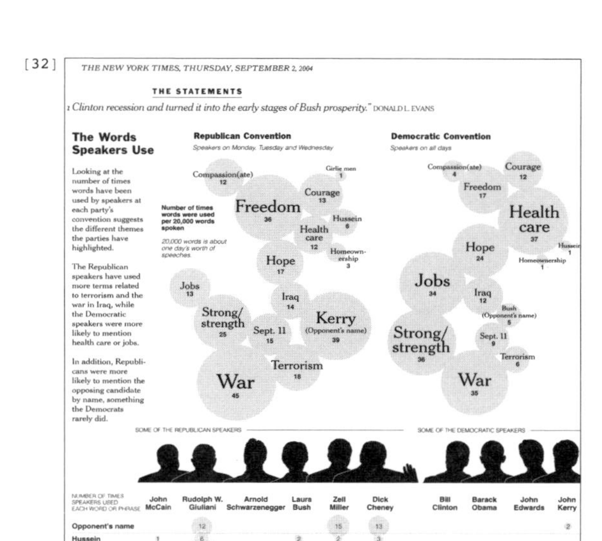

THE NEW YORK TIMES, THURSDAY, SEPTEMBER 2, 2004

THE STATEMENTS

ı Clinton recession and turned it into the early stages of Bush prosperity." DONALD L. EVANS

The Words Speakers Use

Looking at the number of times words have been used by speakers at each party's convention suggests the different themes the parties have highlighted.

The Republican speakers have used more terms related to terrorism and the war in Iraq, while the Democratic speakers were more likely to mention health care or jobs.

In addition, Republicans were more likely to mention the opposing candidate by name, something the Democrats rarely did.

NUMBER OF TIMES SPEAKERS USED EACH WORD OR PHRASE	John McCain	Rudolph W. Giuliani	Arnold Schwarzenegger	Laura Bush	Zell Miller	Dick Cheney	Bill Clinton	Barack Obama	John Edwards	John Kerry
Opponent's name		12			15	13				2
Hussein	1	6		2	2	3				
Terrorism	2	21	2						2	
Religion	1	1	1							1
Afghanistan	1	2		3	2	2	1		1	
Courage	5	1			1	1	1		1	
Homeownership				3		1	1			
Freedom	7	9	4	6	12	7	2	2	2	5
Compassion(ate)			2			1	1			
Sept. 11	4	11		2	1	3	2		3	4
War	18	13		7	8	10	6	6	10	14
Iraq	2	4	3	4	2	3	2	3	9	4
Education		1		4		1			2	3
Strong/strength	2	3	1	4		2	5		5	8
Troops		1	2		2	2		1	1	4
Economy			4			2	3	1	1	3
Hope	1	4	1	4		1		13	8	4
Health care		2		1		1	5	1	9	12
Jobs				1		1	6	5	8	12

Source: Federal News Service transcripts of speeches; Republican National Convention

Matthew Ericson/The New York Times

[33]

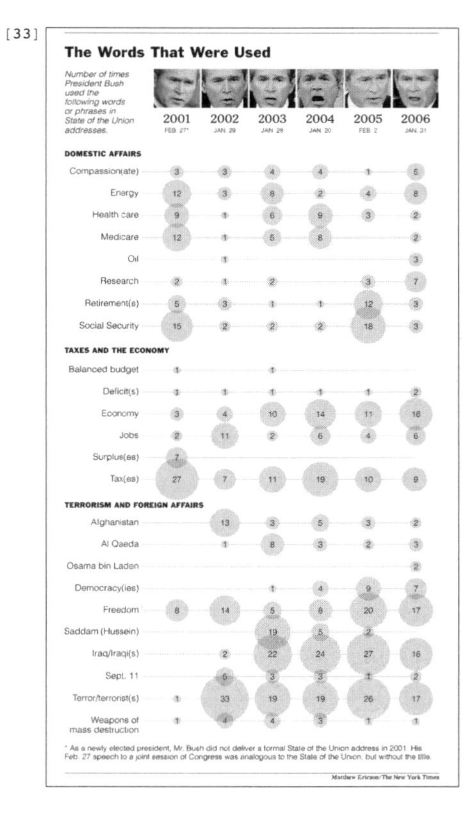

The Words That Were Used

Number of times President Bush used the following words or phrases in State of the Union addresses.

	2001 FEB. 27*	2002 JAN. 29	2003 JAN. 28	2004 JAN. 20	2005 FEB. 2	2006 JAN. 31
DOMESTIC AFFAIRS						
Compassion(ate)	3	3	4	4	1	5
Energy	12	3	8	2	4	8
Health care	9	1	6	9	3	2
Medicare	12	1	5	8		2
Oil		1				3
Research	2	1	2		3	7
Retirement(s)	5	3	1	1	12	3
Social Security	15	2	2	2	18	3
TAXES AND THE ECONOMY						
Balanced budget	1		1			
Deficit(s)	1	1	1	1	1	2
Economy	3	4	10	14	11	16
Jobs	2	11	2	6	4	6
Surplus(es)	7					
Tax(es)	27	7	11	19	10	9
TERRORISM AND FOREIGN AFFAIRS						
Afghanistan		13	3	5	3	2
Al Qaeda		1	8	3	2	3
Osama bin Laden						2
Democracy(ies)			1	4	9	7
Freedom	8	14	5	6	20	17
Saddam (Hussein)			19	5	2	
Iraq/Iraqi(s)		2	22	24	27	16
Sept. 11		5	3	3	1	2
Terror/terrorist(s)	1	33	19	19	26	17
Weapons of mass destruction	1	4	4	3	1	1

* As a newly elected president, Mr. Bush did not deliver a formal State of the Union address in 2001. His Feb. 27 speech to a joint session of Congress was analogous to the State of the Union, but without the title.

Matthew Ericson/The New York Times

The most important thing for us in the graphics department is to create an honest visual impression. We don't want to throw readers a curveball. A good illustration of what we want to avoid is a chart that the Pentagon published in September 2007. [34] This image shows General David Petraeus talking to Brit Hume from Fox News in an interview he gave after he testified before Congress, talking about whether and when there would be troop reductions in Iraq. The chart shown in the background behind General Petraeus conveys a strong visual impression of a downward movement; it looks as if there will be troop reductions at regular intervals over time. But when we got the slide from the Pentagon and looked at it in detail, we found that some of the data isn't quite real: The first two bars of the chart contain actual data; the first bar shows troop numbers as of September of 2006; and the second bar represents the number of troops after the first troop reduction. But the four bars on the right aren't connected to any real data. They're not real projections, because General Petraeus wouldn't say what the reductions would be after the first one.

The scale of the bars is just a fabrication that makes the chart look like it is going down, so you end up with a visual impression of a regular reduction in the troop strength in Iraq, while in reality that hasn't been the case. Since September, General Petraeus has been back in front of Congress twice, both times asking for a delay in deciding whether or not we're going to reduce the troop strength in Iraq. The line should continue to extend horizontally instead of moving downward. While there are caveats about the data printed below the chart, they are only legible when you see it enlarged; it's hard to read them when the graphic is shown on a screen behind someone talking to you on television. At the *New York Times*, we try to prevent this sort of thing by making sure that we don't mix different kinds of data when we create a chart.

[**34**] General David Petraeus, left, talks about force reductions during an interview with Brit Hume on Fox News on September 10, 2007, in Washington. (AP Photo/Kevin Wolf)

[34]

Recommended Force Reductions/Mission Shift
Primary Brigade Mission
Strategic Overwatch
Operational Overwatch
Tactical Overwatch
Partnering
Leading

We also develop numerous maps in our department. A good example of us doing some on-the-ground reporting is a map that we created the Sunday following September 11 [35]; it was one of a series of maps we published following the event. We gathered the data for these maps by sending graphics editors down to Ground Zero, who, sometimes in collaboration with city engineers, determined the status of buildings there. We started out with more of a traditional map, which we published in the early editions of the paper. Later in the day, we tracked down a satellite image taken after the attacks, so we annotated the satellite image, which had more visual power than a traditional map. [36] However, the annotation still draws from the original reporting we did.

This map from 2004 [37] shows donations given to either George Bush or John Kerry from individual addresses in Manhattan. It's great because it gives you an overall impression of the political geography of New York City. As you can see, there are a lot of donations coming for both parties from the Upper East Side, but the Upper West Side is clearly giving more to the Democrats. This is the overall impression you get, but you can also zoom in to see what's happening on your block.

[35] "The Scene of Destruction and the Search for Survivors," *New York Times*, 2001, design: Staff

AFTER THE ATTACKS: Assessing the Damage

The Scene of Destruction ...

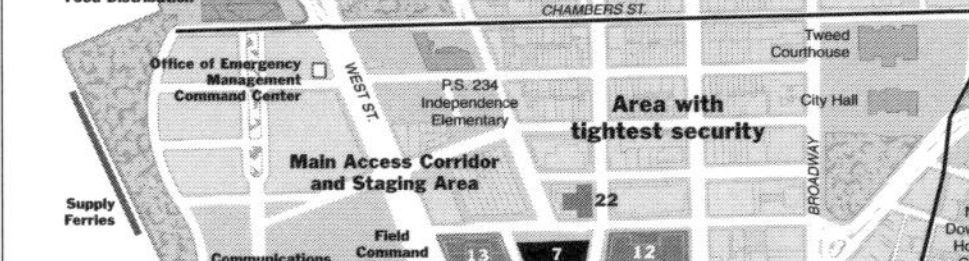

Some Buildings Collapsed or Partially Collapsed

Some Buildings with Major Damage

1. 1 World Trade Center (North Tower)
2. 2 World Trade Center (South Tower)
3. Marriott Hotel
4. 4 World Trade Center
5. 5 World Trade Center
6. 6 World Trade Center
7. 7 World Trade Center
8. North Bridge
9. 1 Liberty Plaza
10. East River Savings Bank
11. Millennium Hilton
12. Federal Building
13. N.Y. Telephone Building
14. Three World Financial Center
15. Two World Financial Center
16. South Bridge
17. One World Financial Center
18. St. Nicholas Greek Orthodox Church
19. 90 West Street
20. Bankers Trust
21. Four World Financial Center
22. 30 West Broadway

... and the Search for Survivors

In times of disaster, the Federal Emergency Management Agency (F.E.M.A.) dispatches its network of Urban Search and Rescue (US&R) teams. They are used to assist local emergency crews in locating victims and managing recovery operations. After the attacks on Tuesday, teams were sent to Manhattan and Washington. The rest are standing by.

HOME BASES *Locations of the US&R teams.*

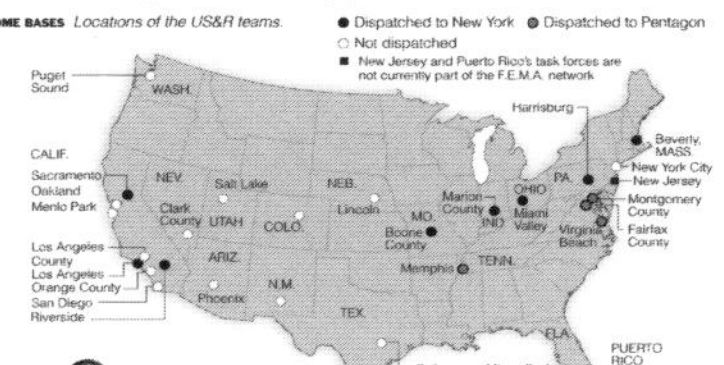

THE MEMBERS *The makeup of the task forces.*

There are 62 members and 4 dogs, divided into two equal groups working 12-hour shifts. The group is made up of emergency medical technicians, including firefighters, paramedics, logistics and communication specialists, structural engineers, doctors, chaplains and K-9 searchers.

THE TASKS *What the task forces do.*

- Perform search and rescue in collapsed buildings.
- Administer initial emergency medical care.
- Deploy search-and-rescue dogs.
- Assess and control gas, electric and hazardous materials.
- Assess and shore up structures as needed.

THE SECTORS

The area has been divided into five sectors. The task forces have been assigned to areas within those sectors.

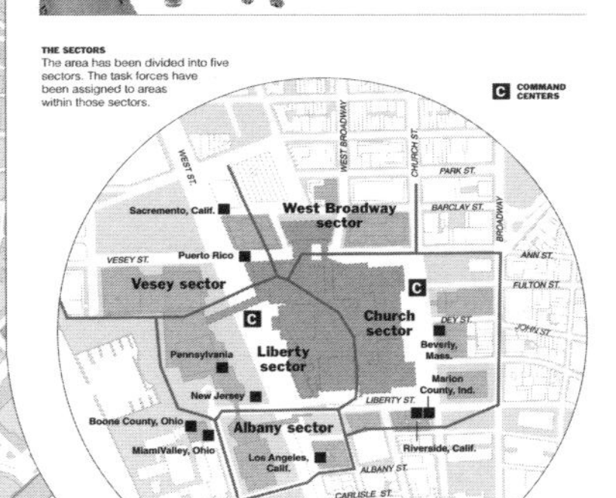

The Effect on the Neighborhood

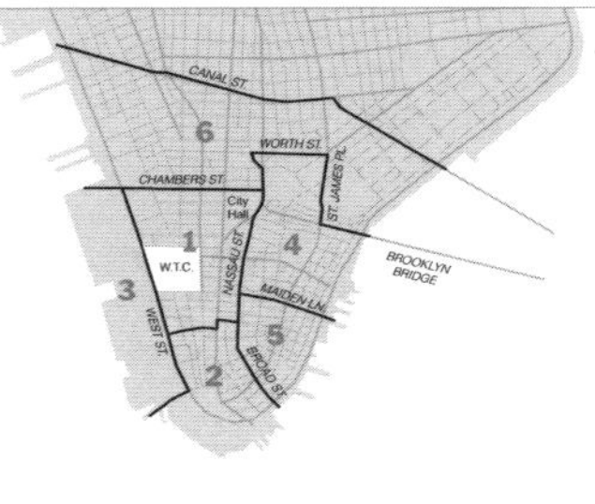

Number of Lower Manhattan Residents Affected by Restrictions *(as of midnight Friday)*

No access to home*	Some access to home with proof of residency	Full access to home with proof of residency
Zone 1 3,130	Zone 2 1,260	Zone 4 .... 9,64(
Zone 3 7,950		Zone 5 2,02
		Zone 6 .... 35,2(

*Some residents of were allowed to retrieve pets and medications.

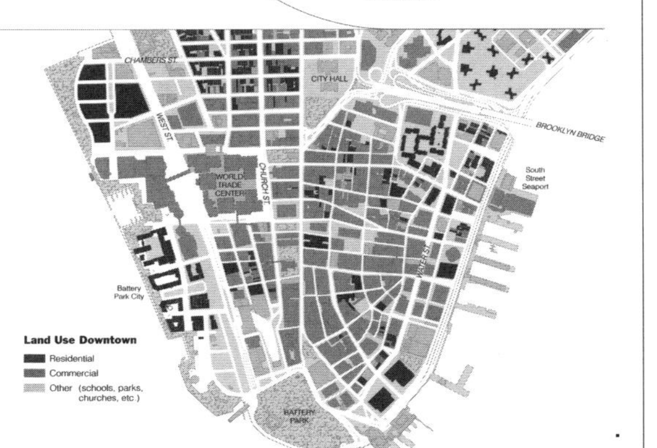

Land Use Downtown

- Residential
- Commercial
- Other (schools, parks, churches, etc.)

Sources: Federal Emergency Management Agency; American Red Cross; New York City Police Department; 2000 Census; Lot Info 2001, Space Track

The New York Times

THE NEW YORK TIMES, SUNDAY, SEPTEMBER 16, 2001

AFTER THE ATTACK: Assessing the Damage

A Look at the Destruction and the Rescue Effort

This satellite image was taken yesterday at 11:54 a.m.

In Presidential Politics, Where the Donors Are

By plotting the addresses of donors to presidential campaigns and the national party committees on a map, patterns of giving emerge. Data from the Federal Election Commission show apartment buildings, offices and other addresses where the occupants have given tens or hundreds of thousands of dollars to support the candidates. *MATTHEW ERICSON*

JOHN KERRY ← **Contributions to each candidate and his party's national committee** → **GEORGE W. BUSH**

and the Democratic National Committee | **and the Republican National Committee**

Manhattan

For both sides, the top ZIP code in the nation for contributions was 10021 on the Upper East Side. Mr. Kerry's appeal, however, was greater throughout much of the rest of Manhattan, bringing in more money than Mr. Bush and the R.N.C. in areas like the Upper West Side, Greenwich Village and SoHo.

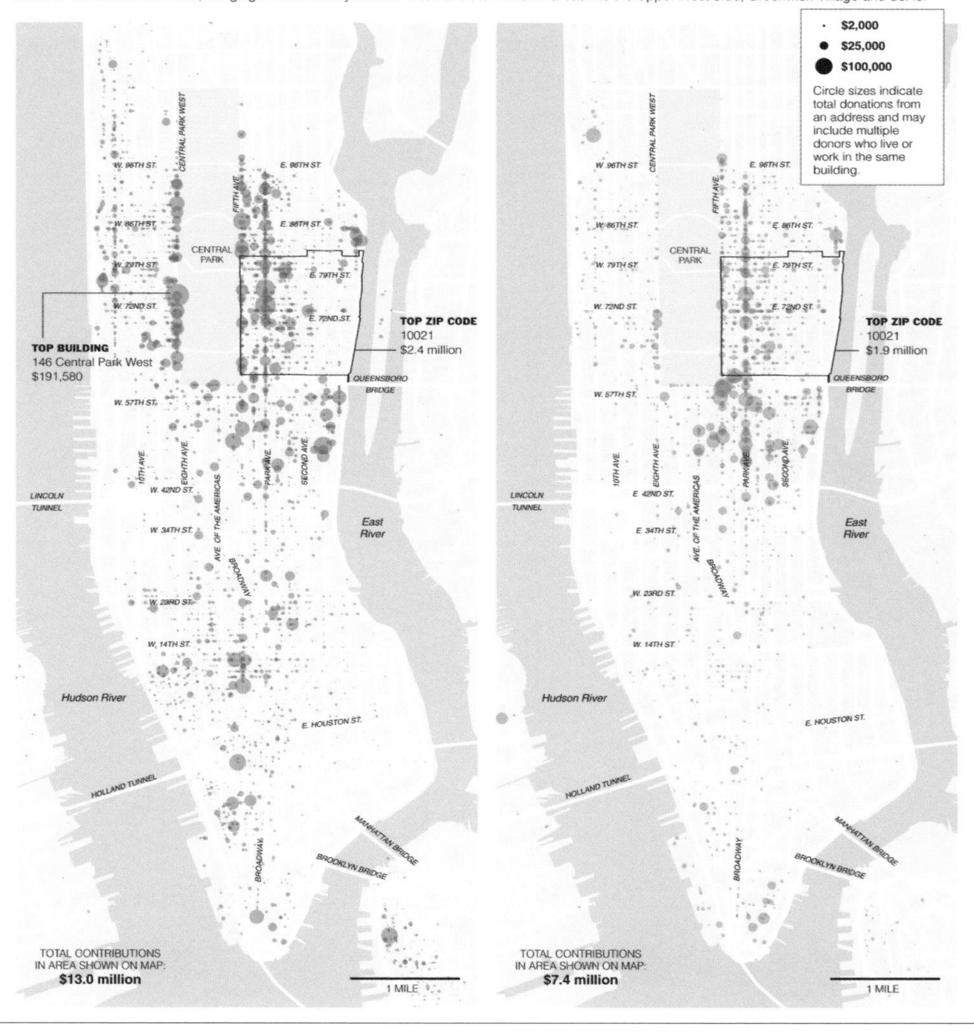

Recently, we've done a lot of primary results mapping. This example shows the Missouri primary results from Super Tuesday. The map illustrates results by county [38], and you can roll over the individual counties to get detailed data. [39] We also presented a margin of victory view. [40] This is important because it shows you how Obama actually won. In the view of results by county, for example, it looks like Clinton has won the state overwhelmingly, but she won mostly in very small counties, and Obama ended up winning the state by picking up a lot of votes in urban counties.

[**38**] "Missouri Primary Results," *New York Times*, 2008, designer: Matthew Bloch [**39**] "Missouri Primary Results," *New York Times*, 2008, designer: Matthew Bloch [**40**] "Missouri Primary Results," *New York Times*, 2008, designer: Matthew Bloch

[38]

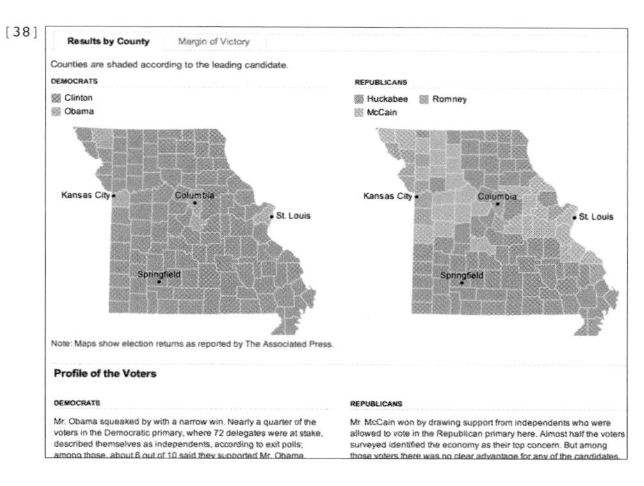

Results by County
Margin of Victory
Counties are shaded according to the leading candidate.
DEMOCRATS
Clinton
Obama
REPUBLICANS
Huckabee
Romney
McCain
Kansas City
Columbia
St. Louis
Springfield
Note: Maps show election returns as reported by The Associated Press.
Profile of the Voters
DEMOCRATS
Mr. Obama squeaked by with a narrow win. Nearly a quarter of the voters in the Democratic primary, where 72 delegates were at stake, described themselves as independents, according to exit polls; among those, about 6 out of 10 said they supported Mr. Obama.
REPUBLICANS
Mr. McCain won by drawing support from independents who were allowed to vote in the Republican primary here. Almost half the voters surveyed identified the economy as their top concern. But among those voters there was no clear advantage for any of the candidates.

[39]

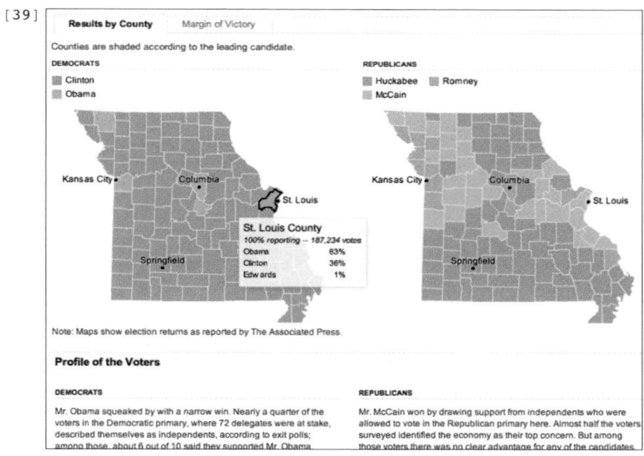

Results by County
Margin of Victory
Counties are shaded according to the leading candidate.
DEMOCRATS
Clinton
Obama
REPUBLICANS
Huckabee
Romney
McCain
Kansas City
Columbia
St. Louis
St. Louis County
100% reporting -- 187,234 votes
Obama 63%
Clinton 36%
Edwards 1%
Springfield
Note: Maps show election returns as reported by The Associated Press.
Profile of the Voters
DEMOCRATS
Mr. Obama squeaked by with a narrow win. Nearly a quarter of the voters in the Democratic primary, where 72 delegates were at stake, described themselves as independents, according to exit polls; among those, about 6 out of 10 said they supported Mr. Obama.
REPUBLICANS
Mr. McCain won by drawing support from independents who were allowed to vote in the Republican primary here. Almost half the voters surveyed identified the economy as their top concern. But among those voters there was no clear advantage for any of the candidates.

[40]

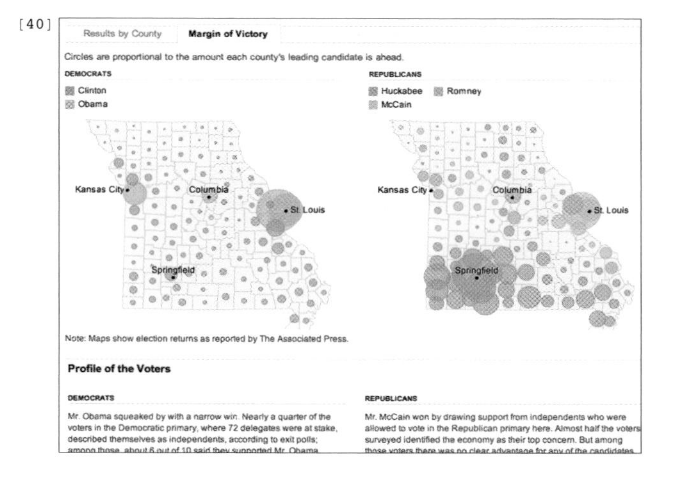

Results by County
Margin of Victory
Circles are proportional to the amount each county's leading candidate is ahead.
DEMOCRATS
Clinton
Obama
REPUBLICANS
Huckabee
Romney
McCain
Kansas City
Columbia
St. Louis
Springfield
Note: Maps show election returns as reported by The Associated Press.
Profile of the Voters
DEMOCRATS
Mr. Obama squeaked by with a narrow win. Nearly a quarter of the voters in the Democratic primary, where 72 delegates were at stake, described themselves as independents, according to exit polls; among those, about 6 out of 10 said they supported Mr. Obama.
REPUBLICANS
Mr. McCain won by drawing support from independents who were allowed to vote in the Republican primary here. Almost half the voters surveyed identified the economy as their top concern. But among those voters there was no clear advantage for any of the candidates.

In this map of the Katrina diaspora [41] we're showing a couple of things. We're trying to give the overall impression of the Katrina diaspora—to illustrate where people from the New Orleans area moved after the hurricane struck. It was known at that time that most of the people moved into the areas surrounding New Orleans, and so the chart obviously shows a fair amount of distortion in that region. But we were interested in presenting a national impression of what the Katrina diaspora looked like. We also wanted to give some details of rural counties in Illinois, Indiana, and Iowa and show just how many people from New Orleans moved there. The data for the map came from FEMA; it shows where aid applications were mailed from.

We create tons of diagrams in the graphics department. This diagram [42] is a visualization of elevation data, accompanying a story about a novice climber going up Kilimanjaro. We gathered the elevation data, extruded it, and projected a satellite image on top of it. We also created a 3-D model of Mount Kilimanjaro, so on the Web, people can follow the climber's route in an animation. [43]

Our goals when creating a diagram are similar to our goals when we make charts and maps. We're not looking to extend the style of the diagram beyond the information we have. We're trying to be clear. This diagram of the stairwells in the north tower of the World Trade Center [44] accompanied the stories of people who were able to make it out. As you can see, it's just a vector line diagram, and not a 3-D rendering. The clearest way was to stick with straight Illustrator drawing (or in this case Adobe Dimensions and Illustrator).

[41] "Katrina's Diaspora," *New York Times*, 2005, designer: Matthew Ericson, Archie Tse

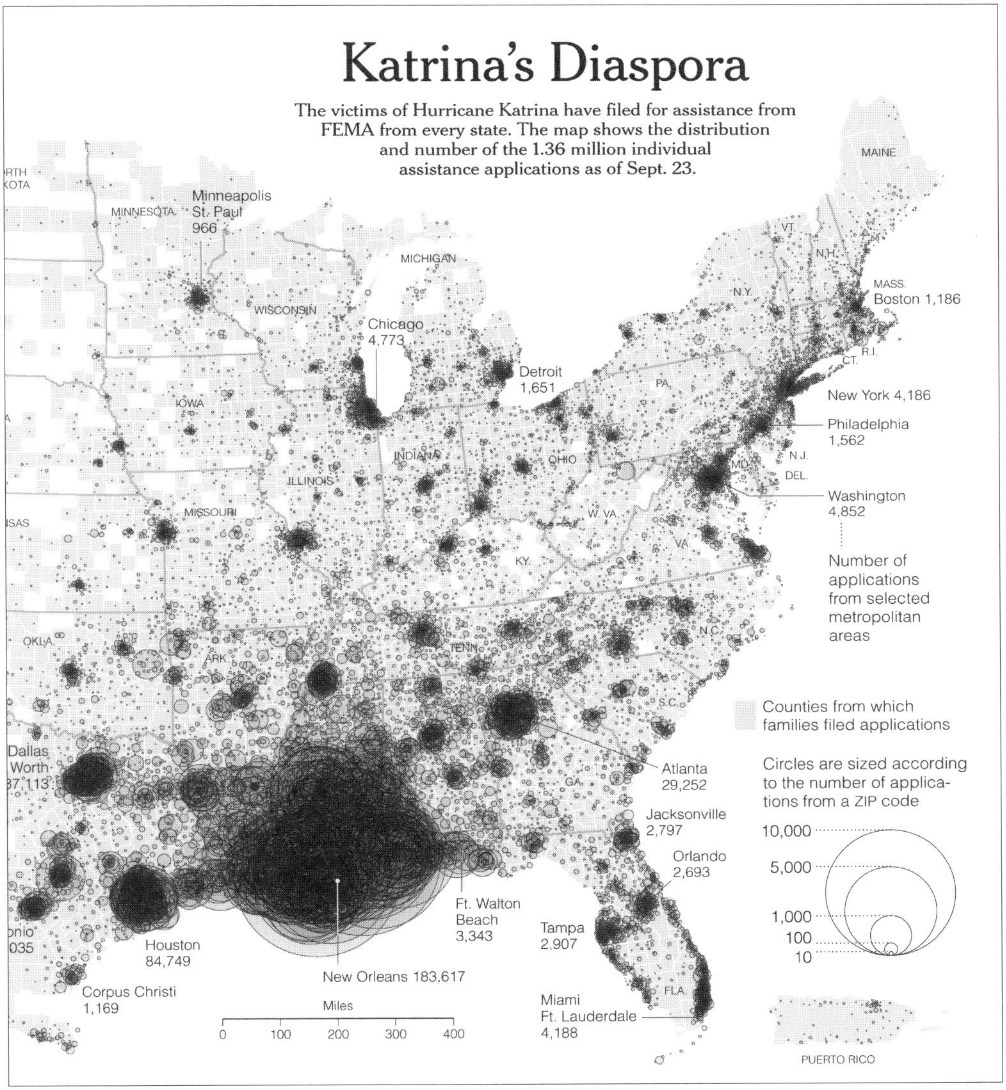

Katrina's Diaspora

The victims of Hurricane Katrina have filed for assistance from FEMA from every state. The map shows the distribution and number of the 1.36 million individual assistance applications as of Sept. 23.

Minneapolis St. Paul 966
Chicago 4,773
Detroit 1,651
Boston 1,186
New York 4,186
Philadelphia 1,562
Washington 4,852
Atlanta 29,252
Jacksonville 2,797
Orlando 2,693
Tampa 2,907
Miami Ft. Lauderdale 4,188
Ft. Walton Beach 3,343
New Orleans 183,617
Houston 84,749
Corpus Christi 1,169
Dallas Worth 37,113
nio 035

MINNESOTA
WISCONSIN
MICHIGAN
IOWA
ILLINOIS
INDIANA
OHIO
MISSOURI
KY.
W. VA.
VA.
PA.
N.Y.
VT.
N.H.
MAINE
MASS.
R.I.
CT.
N.J.
DEL.
MD.
N.C.
S.C.
GA.
FLA.
TENN.
ARK.
OKLA.
PUERTO RICO

Number of applications from selected metropolitan areas

Counties from which families filed applications

Circles are sized according to the number of applications from a ZIP code

10,000
5,000
1,000
100
10

Miles
0 100 200 300 400

[42]

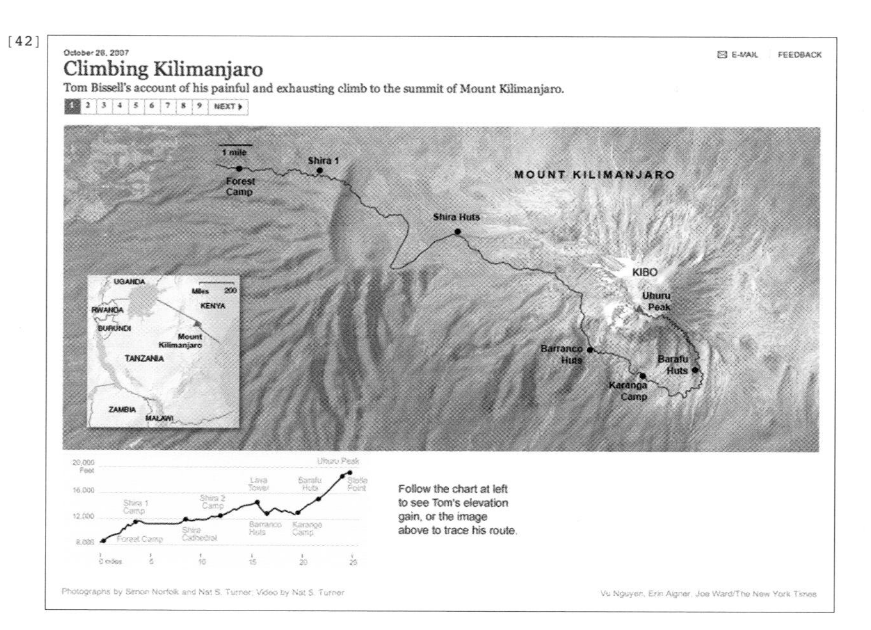

[43]

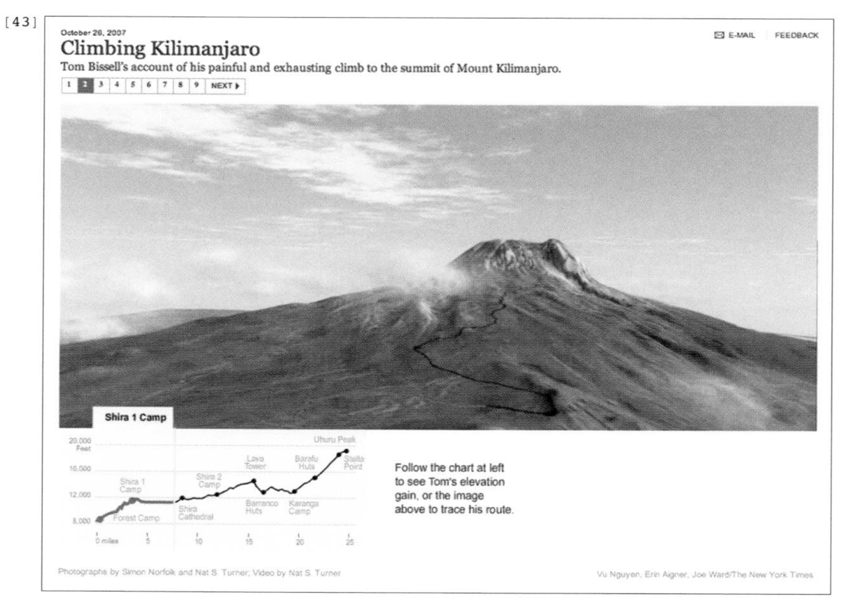

[42] "Climbing Kilimanjaro," *New York Times*, 2005, designer: Vu Nguyen, Erin Aigner, Joe Ward [43] "Climbing Kilimanjaro," *New York Times*, 2005, designer: Vu Nguyen, Erin Aigner, Joe Ward [44] "Inside the North Tower," *New York Times*, 2002, designer: Archie Tse and Steve Duenes

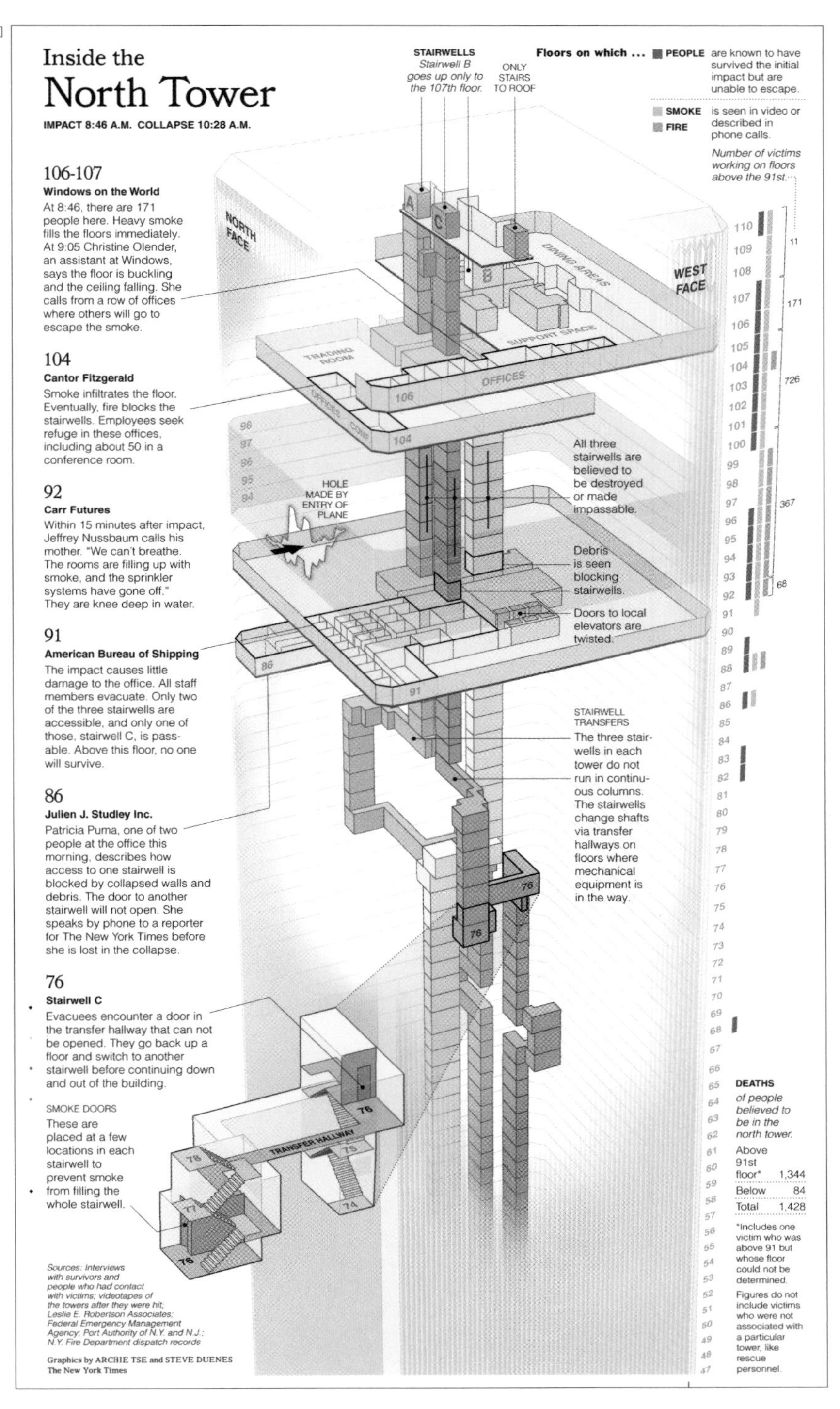

Inside the
North Tower
IMPACT 8:46 A.M. COLLAPSE 10:28 A.M.
106-107
Windows on the World
At 8:46, there are 171 people here. Heavy smoke fills the floors immediately. At 9:05 Christine Olender, an assistant at Windows, says the floor is buckling and the ceiling falling. She calls from a row of offices where others will go to escape the smoke.
104
Cantor Fitzgerald
Smoke infiltrates the floor. Eventually, fire blocks the stairwells. Employees seek refuge in these offices, including about 50 in a conference room.
92
Carr Futures
Within 15 minutes after impact, Jeffrey Nussbaum calls his mother. "We can't breathe. The rooms are filling up with smoke, and the sprinkler systems have gone off." They are knee deep in water.
91
American Bureau of Shipping
The impact causes little damage to the office. All staff members evacuate. Only two of the three stairwells are accessible, and only one of those, stairwell C, is passable. Above this floor, no one will survive.
86
Julien J. Studley Inc.
Patricia Puma, one of two people at the office this morning, describes how access to one stairwell is blocked by collapsed walls and debris. The door to another stairwell will not open. She speaks by phone to a reporter for The New York Times before she is lost in the collapse.
76
Stairwell C
Evacuees encounter a door in the transfer hallway that can not be opened. They go back up a floor and switch to another stairwell before continuing down and out of the building.
SMOKE DOORS
These are placed at a few locations in each stairwell to prevent smoke from filling the whole stairwell.
STAIRWELLS
Stairwell B goes up only to the 107th floor.
ONLY STAIRS TO ROOF
Floors on which ... PEOPLE are known to have survived the initial impact but are unable to escape.
SMOKE is seen in video or
FIRE described in phone calls.
Number of victims working on floors above the 91st.
11
171
726
367
68
NORTH FACE
WEST FACE
A
C
B
DINING AREAS
SUPPORT SPACE
TRADING ROOM
OFFICES
CONF.
106
104
98
97
96
95
94
91
86
HOLE MADE BY ENTRY OF PLANE
All three stairwells are believed to be destroyed or made impassable.
Debris is seen blocking stairwells.
Doors to local elevators are twisted.
STAIRWELL TRANSFERS
The three stairwells in each tower do not run in continuous columns. The stairwells change shafts via transfer hallways on floors where mechanical equipment is in the way.
76
TRANSFER HALLWAY
78
77
75
74
110 109 108 107 106 105 104 103 102 101 100 99 98 97 96 95 94 93 92 91 90 89 88 87 86 85 84 83 82 81 80 79 78 77 76 75 74 73 72 71 70 69 68 67 66 65 64 63 62 61 60 59 58 57 56 55 54 53 52 51 50 49 48 47
DEATHS
of people believed to be in the north tower.
Above 91st floor* 1,344
Below 84
Total 1,428
*Includes one victim who was above 91 but whose floor could not be determined.
Figures do not include victims who were not associated with a particular tower, like rescue personnel.
Sources: Interviews with survivors and people who had contact with victims; videotapes of the towers after they were hit; Leslie E. Robertson Associates; Federal Emergency Management Agency; Port Authority of N.Y. and N.J.; N.Y. Fire Department dispatch records
Graphics by ARCHIE TSE and STEVE DUENES
The New York Times

Obviously, that doesn't mean that we shy away from 3-D renderings. This 3-D diagram [45] describes how a centrifuge works. We had photographic reference material, so we could accurately represent the surfaces and materials of a centrifuge. So even if we choose to do a photo-realistic diagram, we're not inventing anything. We're not going beyond what we know.

The same principle applies to the diagram of Saddam Hussein's hiding place. [46] In this case, a graphics editor who was in Baghdad was able to get on a helicopter, go to the compound, and transmit sketches. We had to create the diagram quickly, and doing it with a rapidograph pen turned out to be the fastest way. It was also the best way to do it without pushing beyond what we knew about the site. Initially, we talked about making a 3-D rendering of the compound, but we really didn't have enough source material. We would have had to invent certain things. We would have had to guess about different materials that existed in different parts of the compound, so we decided that pen and ink was the best way to go.

Applause

MAEDA: Thank you, Steve. Next up, we have Andrew Kuo.

[45] "Spin Cycle," *New York Times*, 2004, designer: Mika Gröndahl
[46] "Hussein's Final Hiding Place," *New York Times*, 2003, designer: Archie Tse, Charles M. Blow, Mika Gröndahl

K

Science Times

N F1

TUESDAY, MARCH 23, 2004

The New York Times

Dr. Lawrence J. Rizzolo asks his anatomy students at Yale to honor their cadavers. One class made a quilt.

George Ruhe for The New York Times

Anatomy Lessons, A Vanishing Rite For Young Doctors

By ABIGAIL ZUGER

Over the centuries, dissecting the human body has evolved from a criminal offense to a vehicle of mass entertainment to an initiation rite.

In the Middle Ages, human dissections were forbidden. In 17th century Europe, medical school dissections were open to the public and often attracted unruly crowds cracking obscene jokes. By the 20th century, dissection had become the exclusive purview of scientists and a mandatory rite of passage for all doctors.

The scandals reported this month with donated cadavers at the University of California, Los Angeles and Tulane University are simply the most recent in a field long beset by abuses.

In 18th and early 19th century America, the public repeatedly rioted against doctors and medical institutions accused of dishonoring the dead. In 1878, the body of Senator John Scott Harrison (the son of President William Henry Harrison) disappeared from its Cincinnati crypt, only to surface in the dissection laboratory of a local medical school.

Now, though, the place of dissection in medical education is changing in ways that have not been seen before.

The hours devoted to formal anatomy training are sharply down in medical schools. Anatomy instructors are in short supply. Computerized scans and three-dimensional recreations of the human body provide cleaner, more colorful teaching tools than the time-consuming dissections of the past.

Some educators say that dissection, as taught to medical students since the Renaissance, is on its way out. Others maintain it is becoming more important than ever, not only for teaching the structure of the human body but also for the more subtle lessons it can impart on the meaning of being a doctor.

"It is always difficult to decide how much anatomy should be learned by a doctor," said Dr. Frank Gonzalez-Crussi, a retired pathologist in Chicago who has written extensively on the history and philosophy of

Continued on Page 6

Douglas Hardy/University of Massachusetts

Prof. Georg Kaser, center, and his team argue that the reasons the ice on Mount Kilimanjaro is melting are complex and should be studied further.

Climate Debate Gets Its Icon: Mt. Kilimanjaro

By ANDREW C. REVKIN

Kilimanjaro, the storied mountain that rises nearly four miles above the shimmering plains of Tanzania, is beginning to resemble the spotted owl — at least in the way it has become a two-sided icon in an environmental debate.

The owl first entered the spotlight 15 years ago, in fierce debate over clear-cutting of ancient Pacific forests. Millions of acres were placed off-limits to logging when the bird was listed as threatened under the federal endangered-species law. Soon afterward, effigies of it began showing up on the grilles of logging trucks.

Kilimanjaro's majestic glacial cap of 11,000-year-old ice has long captured imaginations the world over, so it was not surprising that environmentalists focused their attention on it when scientists reported in 2001 that glaciers around the world were retreating, partly as a result of global warming caused by emissions of heat-trapping "greenhouse" gases from smokestacks and tailpipes.

Campaigners from Greenpeace, the environmental group, scaled the mountain in November 2002 and held a news conference via satellite with reporters at climate-treaty talks in Morocco. Last October, Senator John McCain, the Arizona Republican who is co-author of a bill to curb greenhouse gases, displayed before-and-after photographs of Kilimanjaro during a Senate debate. A British scientist proposed hanging white fabric over the glacier's ragged 10-story-tall edges to block sunlight and stem the erosion.

But now the pendulum has swung. This month, the mountain was taken up as a symbol of eco-alarmism by a cluster of scientists and anti-regulation groups. "Snow Fooling!: Mount Kilimanjaro's glacier retreat is not related to global warming," read a newsletter distribut-

Continued on Page 4

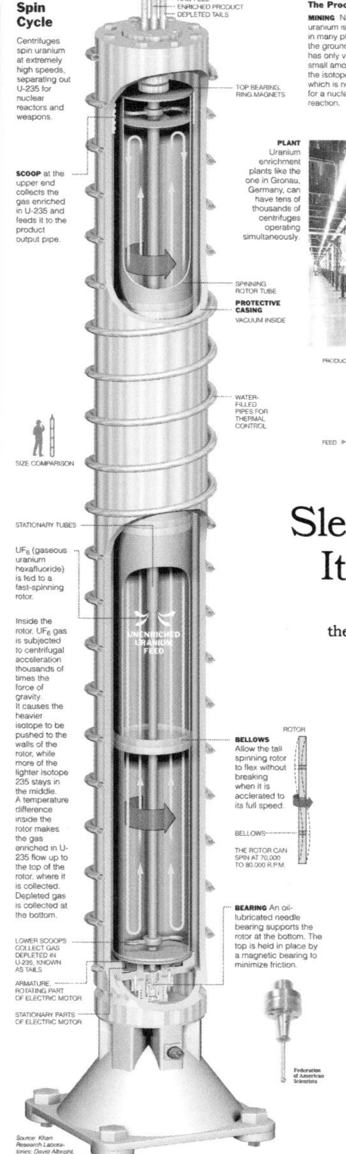
Spin Cycle
Centrifuges spin uranium at extremely high speeds, separating out U-235 for nuclear reactors and weapons.
RAW FEED
ENRICHED PRODUCT
DEPLETED TAILS
TOP BEARING, RING MAGNETS
SCOOP at the upper end collects the gas enriched in U-235 and feeds it to the product output pipe.
SPINNING ROTOR TUBE
PROTECTIVE CASING
VACUUM INSIDE
WATER-FILLED PIPES FOR THERMAL CONTROL
SIZE COMPARISON
STATIONARY TUBES
UF6 (gaseous uranium hexafluoride) is fed to a fast-spinning rotor.
Inside the rotor, UF6 gas is subjected to centrifugal acceleration thousands of times the force of gravity. It causes the heavier isotope to be pushed to the walls of the rotor, while more of the lighter isotope 235 stays in the middle. A temperature difference inside the rotor makes the gas enriched in U-235 flow up to the top of the rotor, where it is collected. Depleted gas is collected at the bottom.
UNENRICHED URANIUM FEED
ROTOR
BELLOWS Allow the tall spinning rotor to flex without breaking when it is acclerated to its full speed.
BELLOWS
THE ROTOR CAN SPIN AT 70,000 TO 80,000 R.P.M.
BEARING An oil-lubricated needle bearing supports the rotor at the bottom. The top is held in place by a magnetic bearing to minimize friction.
LOWER SCOOPS COLLECT GAS DEPLETED IN U-235, KNOWN AS TAILS
ARMATURE, ROTATING PART OF ELECTRIC MOTOR
STATIONARY PARTS OF ELECTRIC MOTOR
Federation of American Scientists

Source: Khan Research Laboratories; David Albright, Institute for Science and International Security

Mika Gröndahl/The New York Times

The Process

MINING Natural uranium is found in many places in the ground, but has only very small amounts of the isotope 235, which is needed for a nuclear reaction.

CONVERSION The raw material from uranium mines is converted into uranium hexafluoride, UF_6.

FLUORIDE

URANIUM

ENRICHMENT The gaseous UF_6 is fed into centrifuges, where the lighter isotope 235 is separated from the heavier 238. The gas is fed through many centrifuges to gain a high level of enrichment.

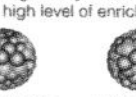
URANIUM 235
URANIUM 238 (THREE ADDITIONAL NEUTRONS)

PLANT Uranium enrichment plants like the one in Gronau, Germany, can have tens of thousands of centrifuges operating simultaneously.

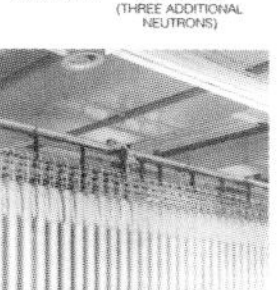

Urenco

PRODUCT

FEED

TAILS

CASCADING To enrich the uranium in significant quantities, many centrifuges are connected to each other to form a cascade. Little by little, the cascade increases the concentrations of U-235.

Slender and Elegant, It Fuels the Bomb

How an Austrian P.O.W. Devised the Machine That Spun the Nuclear Age

By WILLIAM J. BROAD

There was no breakthrough, no eureka, no flash of insight. It happened slowly, the advances gradual until what Dr. Gernot Zippe and his colleagues had invented was a compact, almost elegant device for collecting uranium's rare U-235 isotope.

The feat might have remained obscure, except that it helped define the nuclear era: by the 1960's, Zippe-type machines had become the easiest way to make fuel for reactors as well as weapons of terrifying power, for lighting cities or destroying them.

The invention was the uranium centrifuge, and around the world, millions of them now spin in high-security plants often ringed by barbed wire.

If a chief inventor has any regrets, he keeps them private. In a recent interview, he was philosophical about his team's brainchild, saying nations had the responsibility to determine whether the work would ultimately be judged good or evil.

"With a kitchen knife you can peel a potato or kill your neighbor," Dr. Zippe (pronounced TSIP-eh) said by phone from Munich, where at 86 he still works occasionally and flies off to international meetings. "It's up to governments to use the centrifuge for the benefit of mankind."

And benefits there are. Nuclear reactors, with Zippe-type centrifuges often making their uranium fuel, now generate about 16 percent of the world's electricity. That figure may rise in the decades ahead as worries grow about global warming and oil shortages.

But news of Dr. Zippe's invention has recently centered on the dangers of its illicit spread. Experts warn that it may put nuclear weapons into the hands of terrorists or states sympathetic to them.

Last month, a Pakistani nuclear expert, Abdul Qadeer Khan, admitted running a vast smuggling ring that had supplied at least three nations with Zippe-type centrifuges. It appears to be history's worst case of nuclear proliferation.

While nations congratulate themselves for exposing the network, private experts say the secretive centrifuge design at the heart of the illegal trade is still on the loose and the dangers of its misuse are far from over.

"It's small and you can procure the needed items in secret without being detected," said David Albright, president of the Institute for Science and International Security, an arms control group in Washington. "You end up with a small plant that's very hard to find."

The world may be in for an unsettling time if the future of the Zippe centrifuge is as surprising as its past. The tale of its development is full of striking twists, and no little sweat.

"It was very hard work," said Houston G. Wood, a

Continued on Page 4

THE NEW YORK TIMES **INTERNATIONAL**

THE CAPTURE OF HUSSEIN: 'High-Value Target No. 1'

Hussein's Final Hiding Place: A Small Roadside Compound

AD DWAR, Iraq — Yesterday, allied forces gave a tour of the site where Saddam Hussein was captured, providing a detailed view of the sparse conditions in which he spent his final time as a fugitive. Mr. Hussein was discovered Saturday night hiding in a hole in the ground near a mud hut here. Objects are shown as they were positioned at the time of the tour. *ARCHIE TSE*

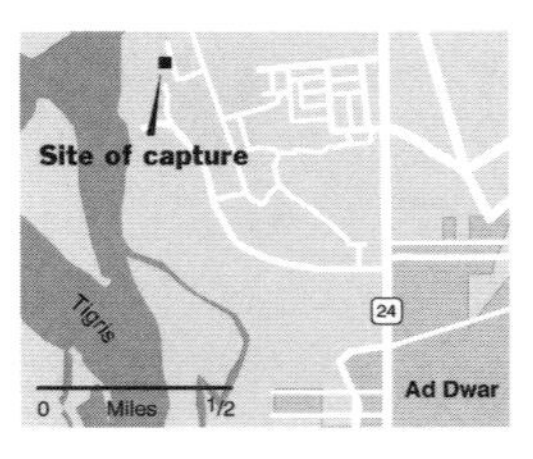

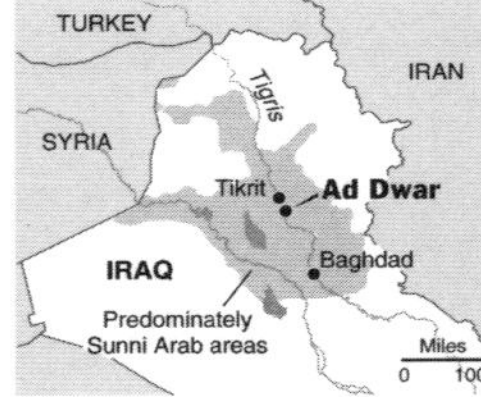

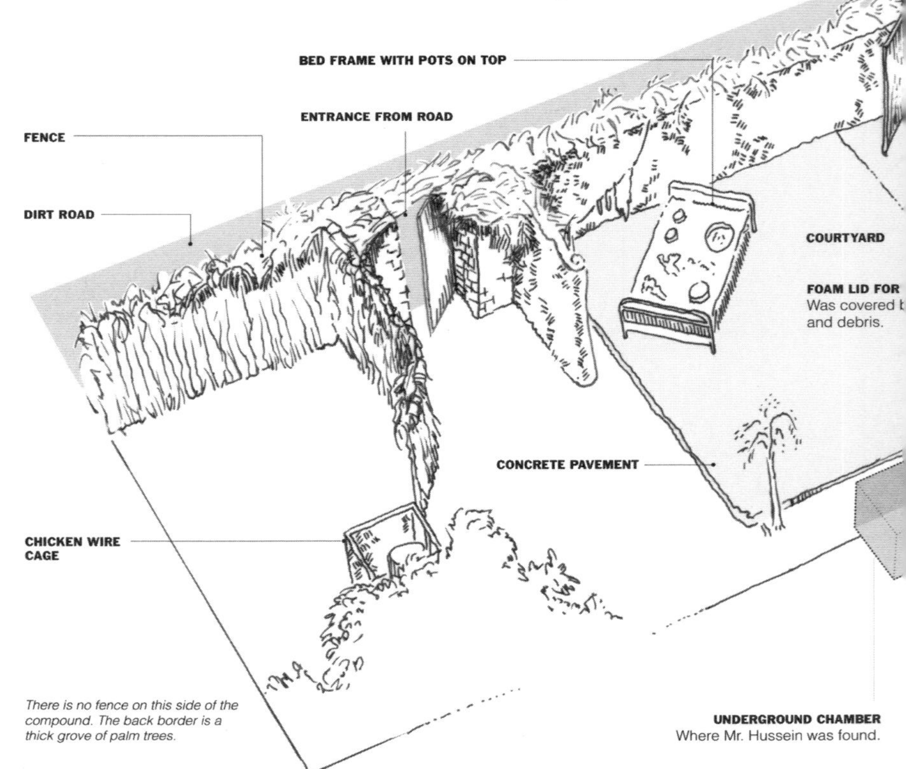

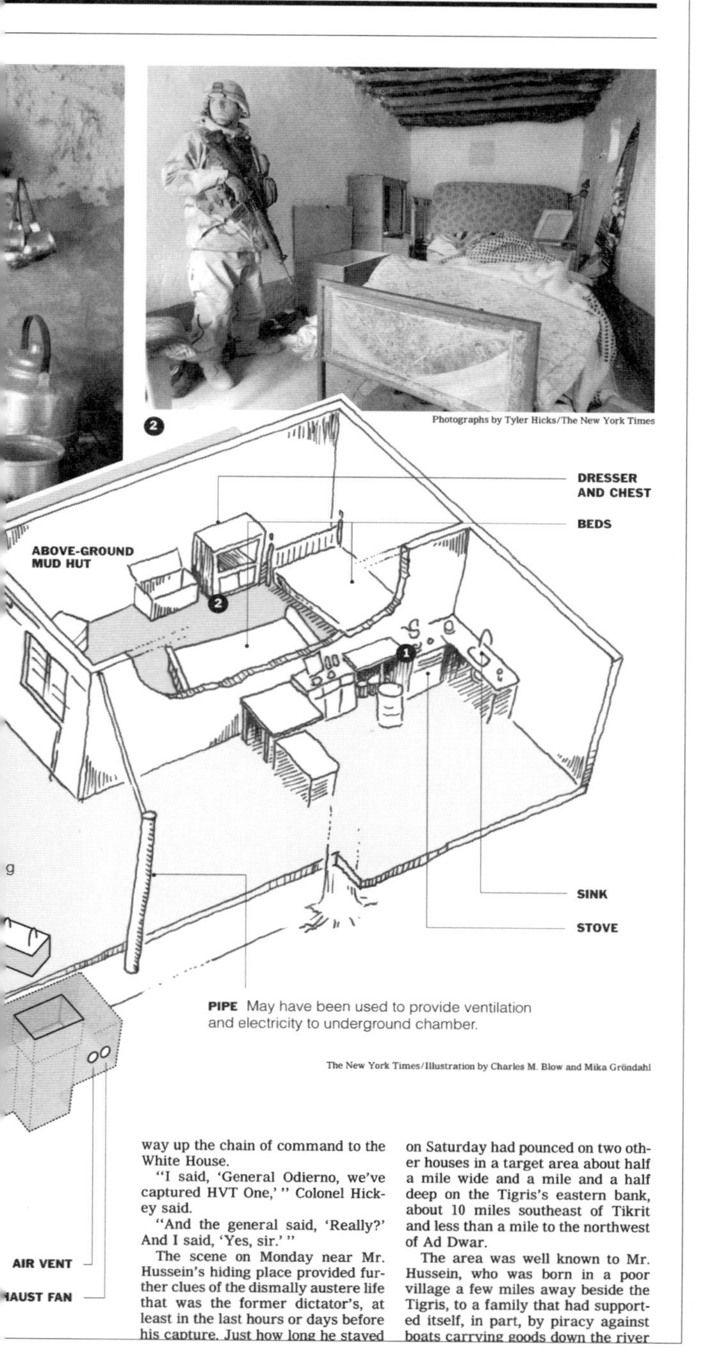

Photographs by Tyler Hicks/The New York Times

The New York Times/Illustration by Charles M. Blow and Mika Gröndahl

way up the chain of command to the White House.

"I said, 'General Odierno, we've captured HVT One,' " Colonel Hickey said.

"And the general said, 'Really?' And I said, 'Yes, sir.' "

The scene on Monday near Mr. Hussein's hiding place provided further clues of the dismally austere life that was the former dictator's, at least in the last hours or days before his capture. Just how long he stayed on Saturday had pounced on two other houses in a target area about half a mile wide and a mile and a half deep on the Tigris's eastern bank, about 10 miles southeast of Tikrit and less than a mile to the northwest of Ad Dwar.

The area was well known to Mr. Hussein, who was born in a poor village a few miles away beside the Tigris, to a family that had supported itself, in part, by piracy against boats carrying goods down the river

Enter

Andrew Kuo

KUO: Hello, my name is Andrew, and I studied at RISD. I found out really quickly that I was no good as a designer, because I was too sloppy and lazy, so I started making art. For about six or seven years now, I've been making handcut paper objects, which are about overcompensating and fear and just trying to conquer this piece of paper. [47] [48] [49] Along the way, I started a blog called earlboykins.blogspot.com. I took that alias because I wanted to psychologically separate this world from my artwork. Earl Boykins's exactly my height—five feet five—and he's a great player for what he is. [50] I started talking about basketball a lot, but one day one of my friends took me to a concert and I sent her a thank-you note in the form of a diagram. I had a lot of fun working on it and realized that I wanted to do more of these and publish them on my blog. So from then on my blog focused on charts of shows that I had seen or of albums I listened to. I'll show you some of them and others tonight.

[47] "All Over Again," 2007, Andrew Kuo [48] "Sooong," 2006, Andrew Kuo
[49] "It's Getting Late," 2006, Andrew Kuo [50] Polaroid by Jason Nocito

[47]

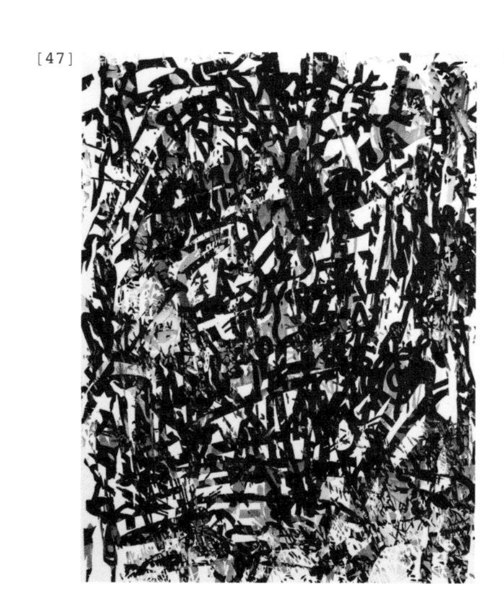

[48]

[49]

[50]

In 2007 I charted the CMJ Music Marathon. I like this diagram [51] a lot because it makes your eyes go cross-eyed. As you can see, my mood got increasingly better toward the end of the CMJ.

The diagram of Deerhunter at Cake Shop [52] has ridiculously large color bars on the bottom that serve as a kind of key to the chart. The show got worse toward the end.

The Health chart [53] is an example of my simple X-axis diagrams, in which I label feelings that I experience during a concert or while listening to an album. On the left is the beginning of the show or album, and the right is the end. As you can see, it was an okay show.

The chart of a Hurricane Chris tape [54] was inspired by my friend Brian Chippendale's book *Maggots*, which reads like a snake, in a zigzag pattern from left to right, and right to left. I started playing around with this pattern, using the same theme as before. It's a really good tape.

[51] "My CMJ Mood During the Course of 4 Days," www.earlboykins.blogspot.com, 2006, Andrew Kuo [52] "Deerhunter At Cakeshop," www.earlboykins.blogspot.com, 2007, Andrew Kuo

[51]

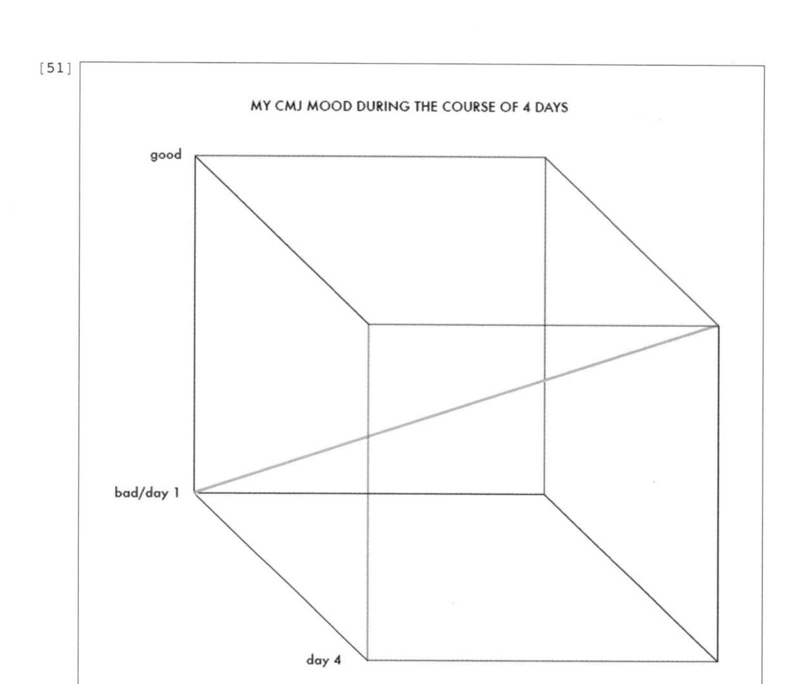
MY CMJ MOOD DURING THE COURSE OF 4 DAYS
good
bad/day 1
day 4

[52]

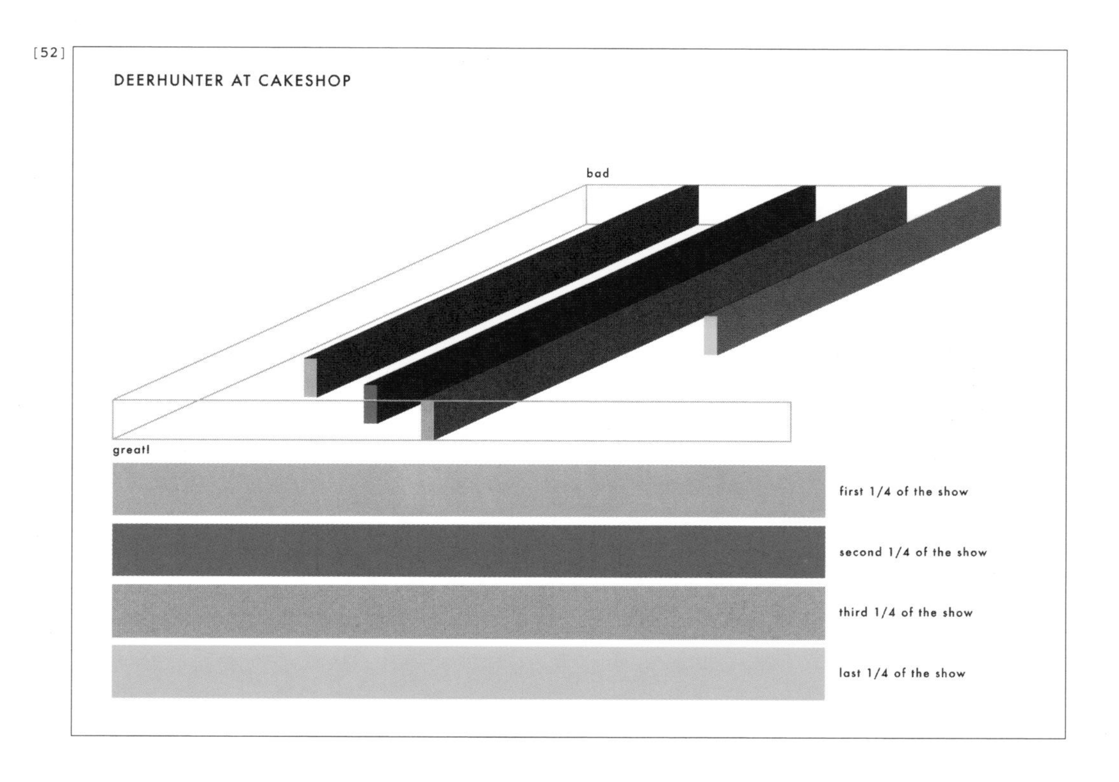
DEERHUNTER AT CAKESHOP
bad
great!
first 1/4 of the show
second 1/4 of the show
third 1/4 of the show
last 1/4 of the show

HEALTH

duration of show ⟶

duration of album ⟶
Fucking awesome! Everything you like about heavy beats, computers, and weirdness all in one!
Kind of really good!
Kind of good! [but i wish it either went nowhere or somewhere... it's stuck in-between]
Another band that swears by the Boredoms. You know the drill by now.
At times like this I wish i was listening to Yo Gotti.

[53]

[53] "Health," www.earlboykins.blogspot.com, 2007, Andrew Kuo

[54]

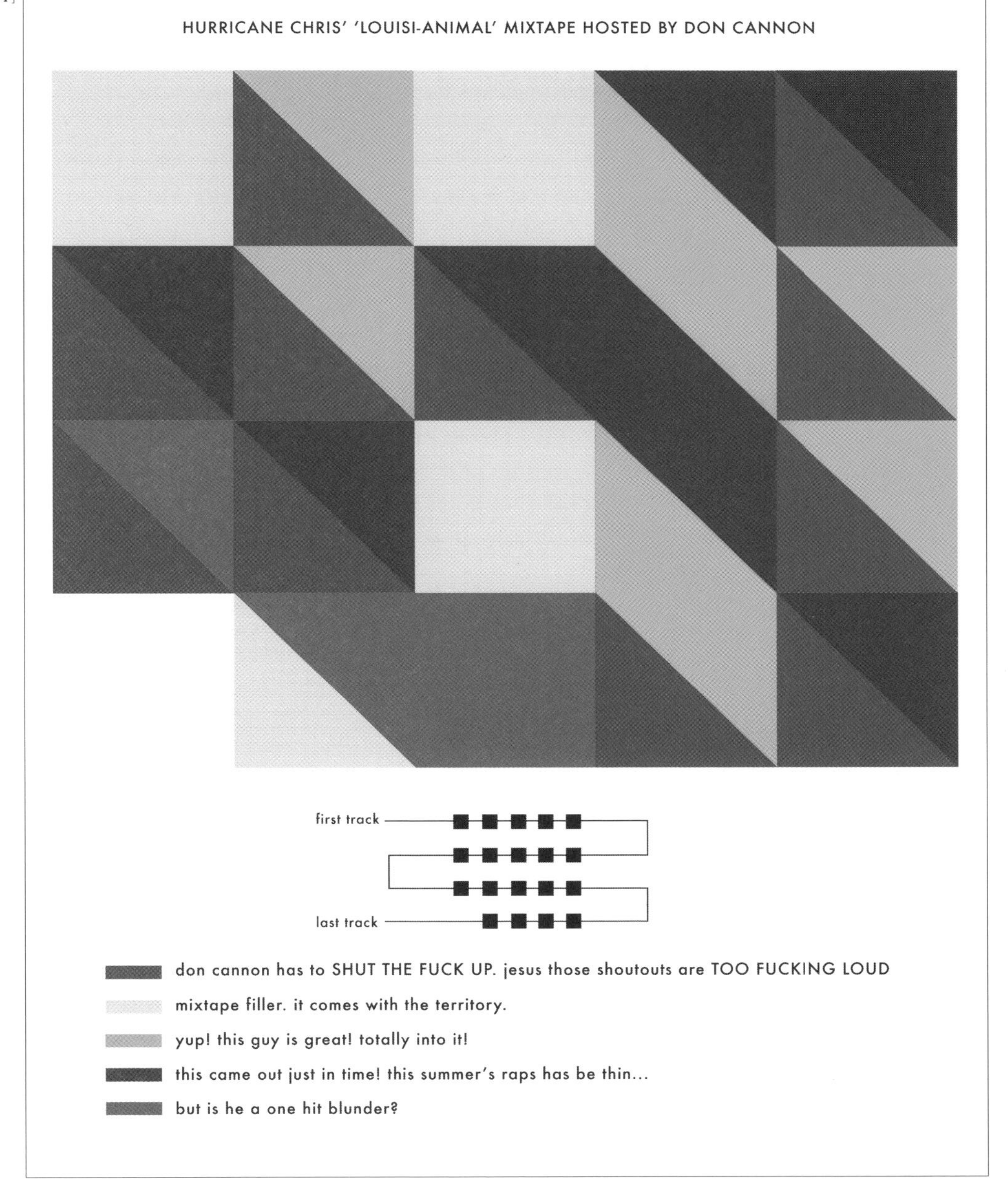
HURRICANE CHRIS' 'LOUISI-ANIMAL' MIXTAPE HOSTED BY DON CANNON
first track
last track
don cannon has to SHUT THE FUCK UP. jesus those shoutouts are TOO FUCKING LOUD
mixtape filler. it comes with the territory.
yup! this guy is great! totally into it!
this came out just in time! this summer's raps has be thin...
but is he a one hit blunder?

[54] "Hurricane Chris' 'Louisi-Animal' Mixtape Hosted by Don Cannon," www.earlboykins.blogspot.com, 2007, Andrew Kuo

The next diagram [55], which illustrates another CMJ show, is getting a bit weird, meaning it's not really working, but that's why I like it. It was a weird show. I don't like Dan Deacon.

Laughs

The Animal Collective diagram [56] is an example of how extraneous you can get with these graphs. The information reads from left to right, like in the Health diagram. But here the data is extruded, which can confuse people, and I like that. It's also totally unnecessary.

Laughs

The watermelon slices at the top of the Atlas Sound chart [57] serve as the key to the diagram, but they're also meant to throw you off. Basically, this chart is a bar graph done in a really bad way. It was a lot of fun to make.

Laughs

This diagram [58] shows Animal Collective in a concert where they stopped in the middle of their set. It is another example of the left-to-right charts, which start at one point and end on another, but this one is bent into a circle. It was a disappointing show.

[55] "The Feel-Good Then Feel-Bad Weirdo Music CMJ Showcase at Bowery Ballroom," www.earlboykins.blogspot.com, 2007, Andrew Kuo

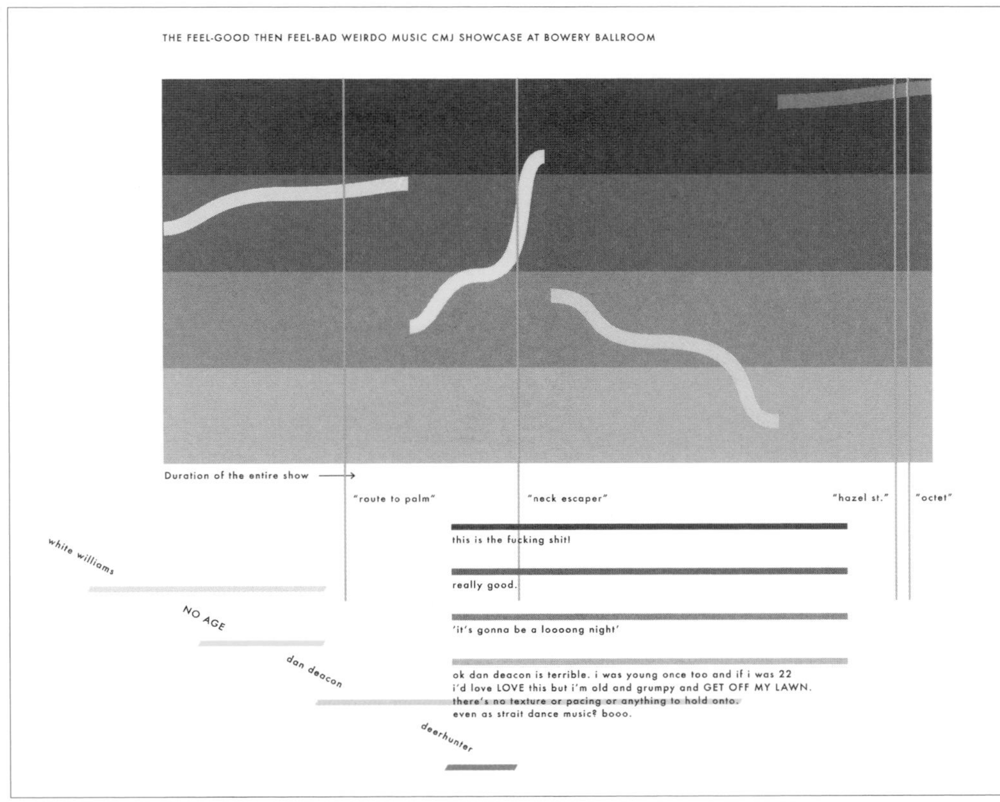
THE FEEL-GOOD THEN FEEL-BAD WEIRDO MUSIC CMJ SHOWCASE AT BOWERY BALLROOM
Duration of the entire show
"route to palm"
"neck escaper"
"hazel st."
"octet"
white williams
NO AGE
dan deacon
deerhunter
this is the fucking shit!
really good.
'it's gonna be a loooong night'
ok dan deacon is terrible. i was young once too and if i was 22
i'd love LOVE this but i'm old and grumpy and GET OFF MY LAWN.
there's no texture or pacing or anything to hold onto.
even as strait dance music? booo.

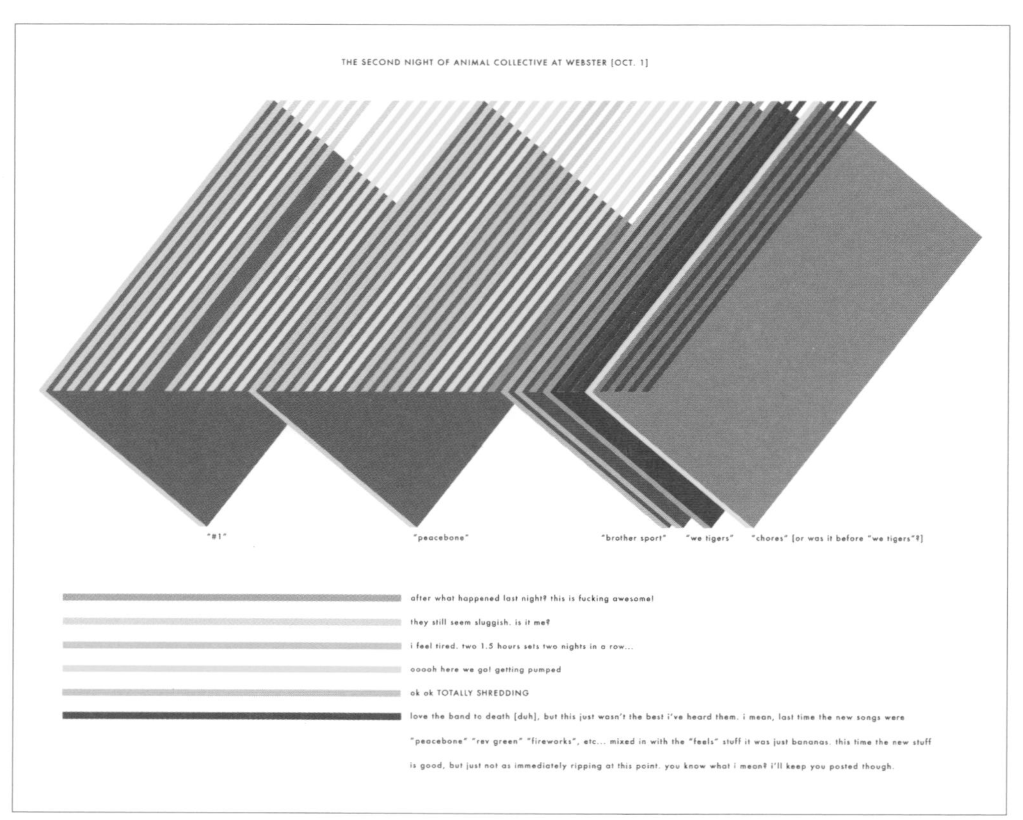
THE SECOND NIGHT OF ANIMAL COLLECTIVE AT WEBSTER [OCT. 1]
"#1"
"peacebone"
"brother sport"
"we tigers"
"chores" [or was it before "we tigers"?]
after what happened last night? this is fucking awesome!
they still seem sluggish. is it me?
i feel tired. two 1.5 hours sets two nights in a row...
ooooh here we go! getting pumped
ok ok TOTALLY SHREDDING
love the band to death [duh], but this just wasn't the best i've heard them. i mean, last time the new songs were
"peacebone" "rev green" "fireworks", etc... mixed in with the "feels" stuff it was just bananas. this time the new stuff
is good, but just not as immediately ripping at this point. you know what i mean? i'll keep you posted though.

[56]

[56] "The Second Night of Animal Collective at Webster [Oct. 1]," www.earlboykins.blogspot.com, 2007, Andrew Kuo [57] "Atlas Sound," www.earlboykins.blogspot.com, 2007, Andrew Kuo [58] "The First Night of Animal Collective at Webster [Nov. 30]," www.earlboykins.blogspot.com, 2007, Andrew Kuo

[57]

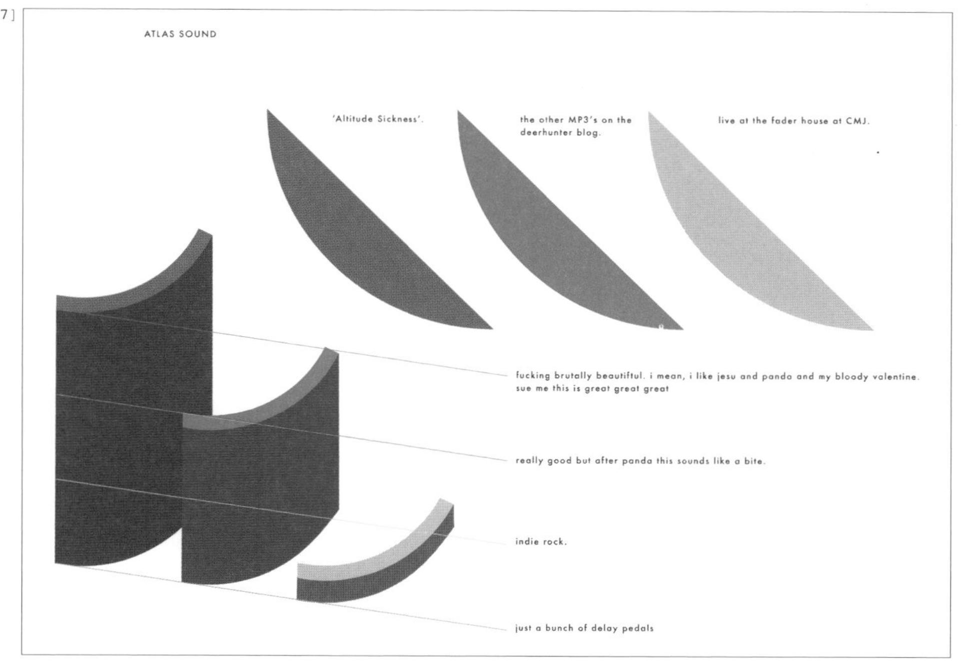
ATLAS SOUND
'Altitude Sickness'.
the other MP3's on the deerhunter blog.
live at the fader house at CMJ.
fucking brutally beautiftul. i mean, i like jesu and panda and my bloody valentine. sue me this is great great great
really good but after panda this sounds like a bite.
indie rock.
just a bunch of delay pedals

[58]

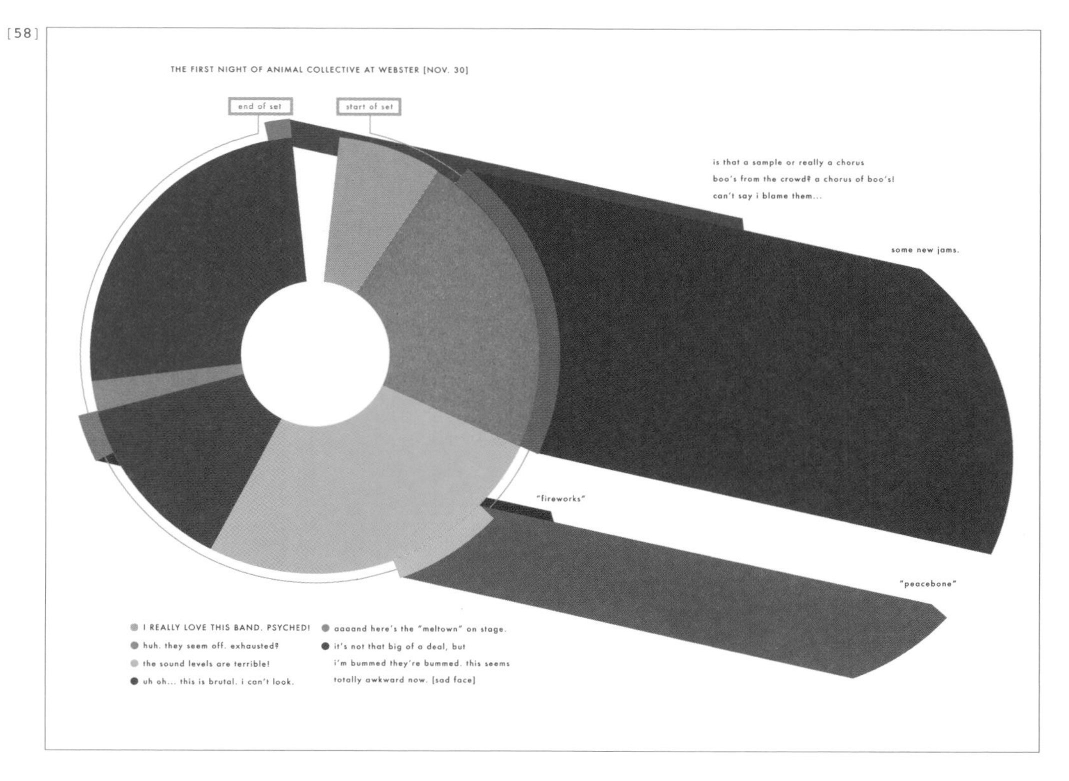
THE FIRST NIGHT OF ANIMAL COLLECTIVE AT WEBSTER [NOV. 30]
end of set
start of set
is that a sample or really a chorus
boo's from the crowd? a chorus of boo's!
can't say i blame them...
some new jams.
"fireworks"
"peacebone"
I REALLY LOVE THIS BAND. PSYCHED!
huh. they seem off. exhausted?
the sound levels are terrible!
uh oh... this is brutal. i can't look.
aaaand here's the "meltown" on stage.
it's not that big of a deal, but i'm bummed they're bummed. this seems totally awkward now. [sad face]

The next image [59] is really important to me. I think I find myself standing here in front of you because I used to collect baseball cards when I was little and I would sit for hours and hours just creating different piles of cards and categorizing them. I would create different systems every day. Before dinner, I would make a pile of all my favorite teams. Then I'd come back from dinner and make, with those same cards, a different pile based on which cards I wanted to trade or which players I didn't like. I think that had a lot to do with the way I think about art. To me, it's all about organizing, separating, and editing. This is an awesome card, by the way. It was worth $80 at one point.

Around 2007 I started working for the *New York Times*. They contacted me about charting seven nights of Bright Eyes shows in a week [60], which I'm sure sounds like a nightmare to many of you but is kind of my fantasy. I really, really enjoyed it. Being a fan inspires me to do these extraneous things, because I just can't help but tell everyone how much I loved a show or hated it. Enthusiasm is a big part of what I do. This happiness or sadness you feel makes you take that extra step.

[59] Billy Ripken, Fleer, 1989 **[60]** "7 Nights of Bright Eyes (in as Many Colors)," *New York Times*, 2007, Andrew Kuo

[59]

BILL RIPKEN
SECOND BASE
FLEER

[60]

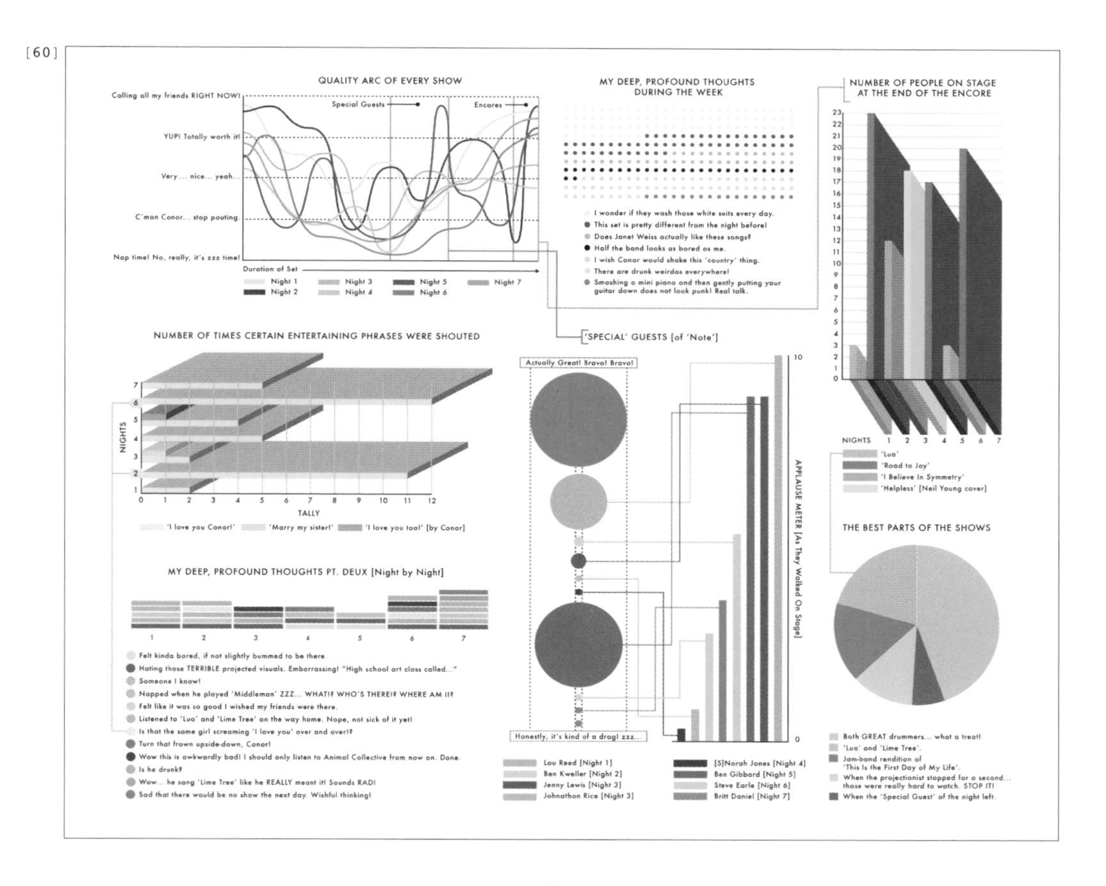
QUALITY ARC OF EVERY SHOW
Calling all my friends RIGHT NOW!
YUP! Totally worth it!
Very.... nice... yeah...
C'mon Conor... stop pouting.
Nap time! No, really, it's zzz time!
Special Guests
Encores
Duration of Set
Night 1
Night 2
Night 3
Night 4
Night 5
Night 6
Night 7
MY DEEP, PROFOUND THOUGHTS DURING THE WEEK
I wonder if they wash those white suits every day.
This set is pretty different from the night before!
Does Janet Weiss actually like these songs?
Half the band looks as bored as me.
I wish Conor would shake this 'country' thing.
There are drunk weirdos everywhere!
Smashing a mini piano and then gently putting your guitar down does not look punk! Real talk.
NUMBER OF PEOPLE ON STAGE AT THE END OF THE ENCORE
NIGHTS 1 2 3 4 5 6 7
'Lua'
'Road to Joy'
'I Believe In Symmetry'
'Helpless' [Neil Young cover]
NUMBER OF TIMES CERTAIN ENTERTAINING PHRASES WERE SHOUTED
NIGHTS
TALLY
'I love you Conor!'
'Marry my sister!'
'I love you too!' [by Conor]
'SPECIAL' GUESTS [of 'Note']
Actually Great! Bravo! Bravo!
Honestly, it's kind of a drag! zzz...
APPLAUSE METER [As They Walked On Stage]
Lou Reed [Night 1]
Ben Kweller [Night 2]
Jenny Lewis [Night 3]
Johnathon Rice [Night 3]
[S]Norah Jones [Night 4]
Ben Gibbard [Night 5]
Steve Earle [Night 6]
Britt Daniel [Night 7]
MY DEEP, PROFOUND THOUGHTS PT. DEUX [Night by Night]
Felt kinda bored, if not slightly bummed to be there.
Hating those TERRIBLE projected visuals. Embarrassing! "High school art class called..."
Someone I know!
Napped when he played 'Middleman' ZZZ... WHAT!? WHO'S THERE!? WHERE AM I!?
Felt like it was so good I wished my friends were there.
Listened to 'Lua' and 'Lime Tree' on the way home. Nope, not sick of it yet!
Is that the same girl screaming 'I love you' over and over!?
Turn that frown upside-down, Conor!
Wow this is awkwardly bad! I should only listen to Animal Collective from now on. Done.
Is he drunk?
Wow... he sang 'Lime Tree' like he REALLY meant it! Sounds RAD!
Sad that there would be no show the next day. Wishful thinking!
THE BEST PARTS OF THE SHOWS
Both GREAT drummers... what a treat!
'Lua' and 'Lime Tree'.
Jam-band rendition of 'This Is the First Day of My Life'.
When the projectionist stopped for a second... those were really hard to watch. STOP IT!
When the 'Special Guest' of the night left.

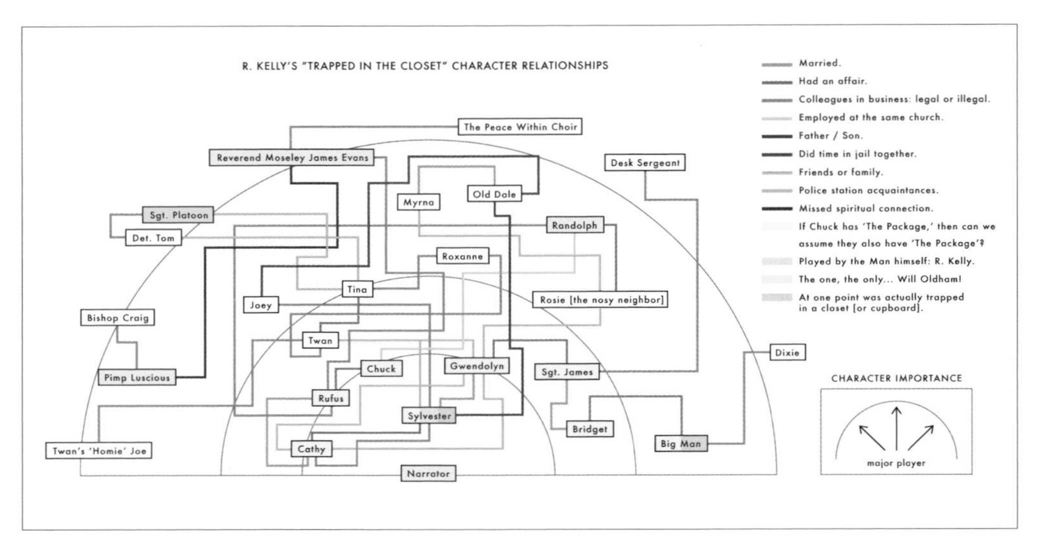

[61]

[61] "Someone's in the Closet with Sylvester," *New York Times*, 2007, Andrew Kuo [62] "Character Appearances by Chapter," *New York Times*, 2007, Andrew Kuo

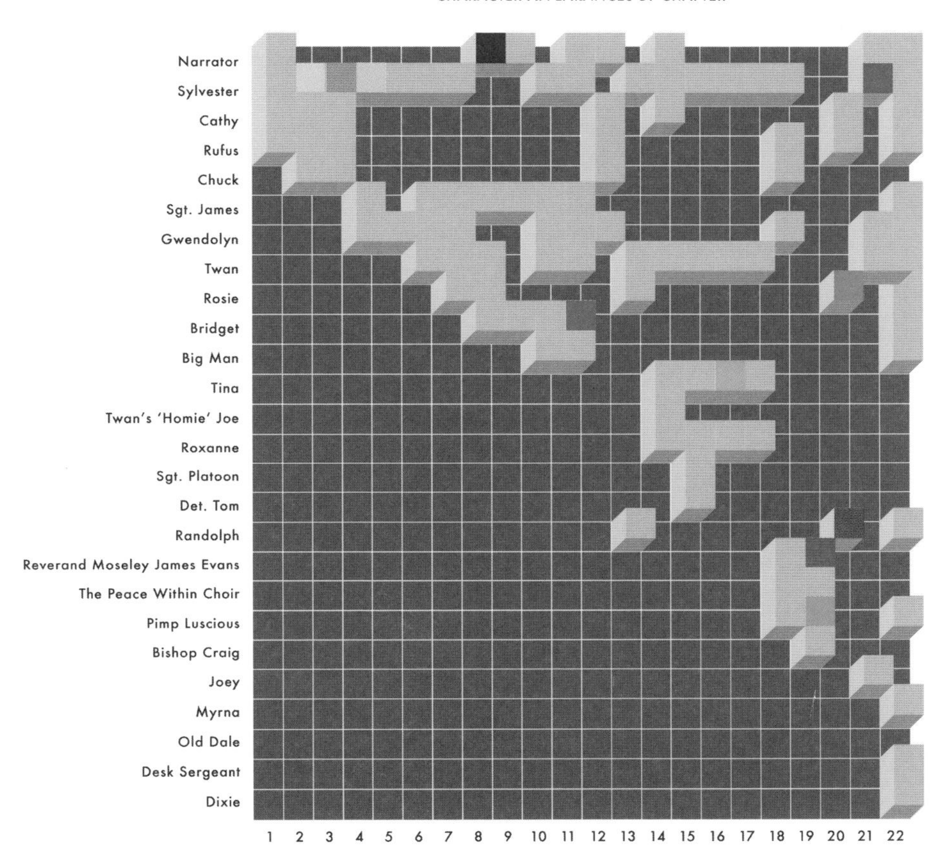

MEMORABLE QUOTES

- "Your trick chose me!"
- "I can't believe it's a man, man, man."
- "Oh my god! A rubber, rubber, rubber." [does this set up an AIDS bombshell?]
- "Then he notices the pie on the counter... one slice is missing... Bridget's allergic to cherries."
- "Not only have I been sleeping with Big Man, he's my baby's daddy."
- "He's got the radio bumping Mary J."
- "Stop pimpin'!"
- "P-P-Pimpin's for life!"
- "I'm gonna slap you with this hot water bag if you don't start talking to me!"
- "HE [Rufus] GOT THE 'PACKAGE'!"
- "Joey, I'm telling you, you could own your own pasta factory."

I made two diagrams of R. Kelly's urban opera *Trapped in the Closet* for the *New York Times*. They actually pay me for these things. The first diagram [61] shows how all the characters are connected, with Sylvester, the narrator, in the middle. I actually made a mistake in the chart and color-coded two characters wrong.

The second *Trapped in the Closet* graph [62] shows which characters appear in which episodes or chapters. I find that you can make a hundred charts and then suddenly one will visually make sense, and this is one of the ones. I've only made about three charts where the visualization of the data is really informing me of something I did not know before I made it.

Last summer I covered the McCarren Park Pool concerts in Williamsburg, Brooklyn. The disappointment of missing Superchunk inspired me to do this chart. [63] I was really heartbroken about it, but it fueled me to make a diagram. It's weird how emotions such as disappointment can inspire you. Among other things, you can see what my moods were during the show, why I think people came to the concerts, and pyramids of highs and lows.

[63] "No Life Guard on Duty," *New York Times*, 2007, Andrew Kuo

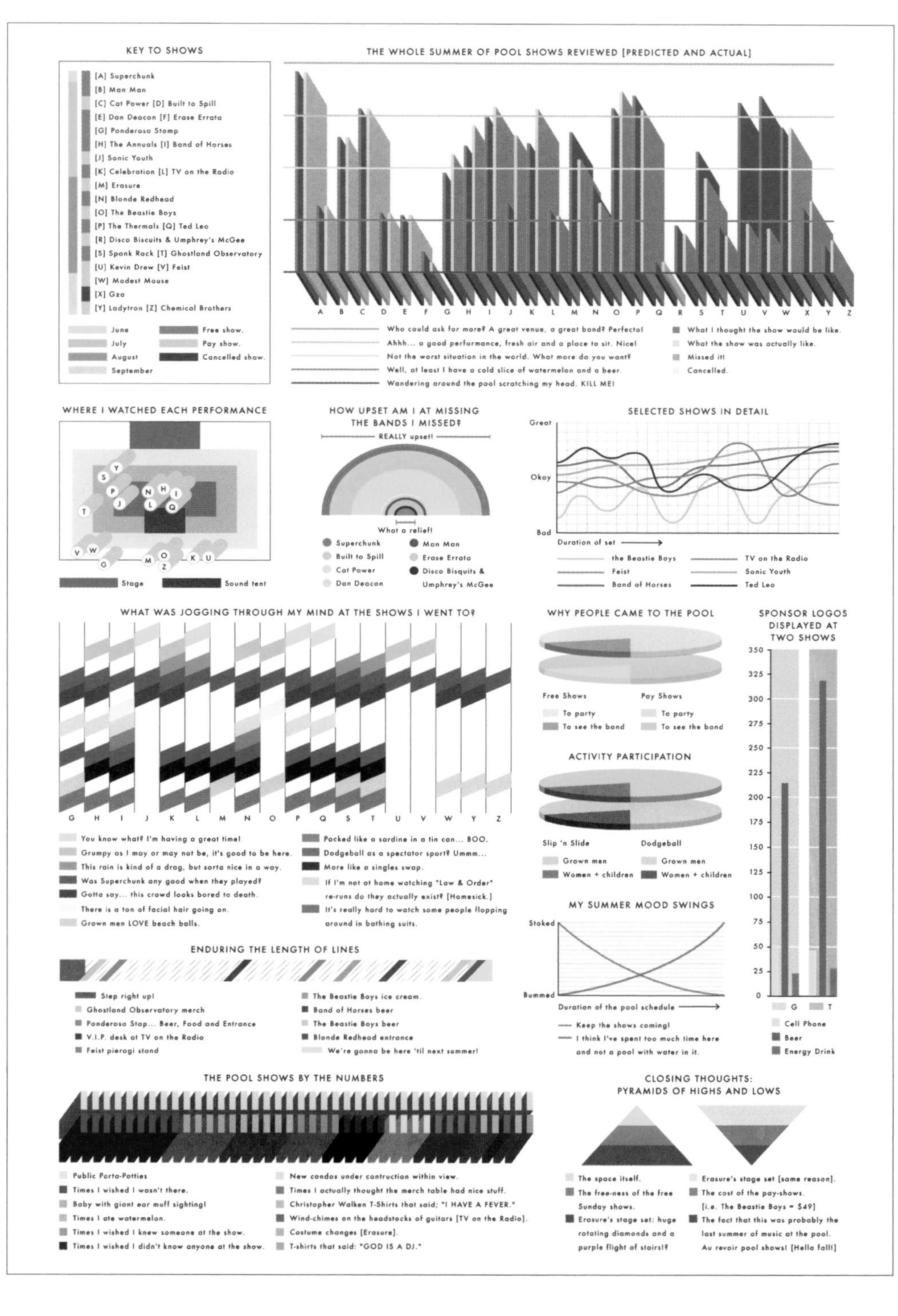
KEY TO SHOWS
[A] Superchunk
[B] Man Man
[C] Cat Power [D] Built to Spill
[E] Dan Deacon [F] Erase Errata
[G] Ponderosa Stomp
[H] The Annuals [I] Band of Horses
[J] Sonic Youth
[K] Celebration [L] TV on the Radio
[M] Erasure
[N] Blonde Redhead
[O] The Beastie Boys
[P] The Thermals [Q] Ted Leo
[R] Disco Biscuits & Umphrey's McGee
[S] Spank Rock [T] Ghostland Observatory
[U] Kevin Drew [V] Feist
[W] Modest Mouse
[X] Gza
[Y] Ladytron [Z] Chemical Brothers
June
July
August
September
Free show.
Pay show.
Cancelled show.
THE WHOLE SUMMER OF POOL SHOWS REVIEWED [PREDICTED AND ACTUAL]
A B C D E F G H I J K L M N O P Q R S T U V W X Y Z
Who could ask for more? A great venue, a great band? Perfecto!
Ahhh... a good performance, fresh air and a place to sit. Nice!
Not the worst situation in the world. What more do you want?
Well, at least I have a cold slice of watermelon and a beer.
Wandering around the pool scratching my head. KILL ME!
What I thought the show would be like.
What the show was actually like.
Missed it!
Cancelled.
WHERE I WATCHED EACH PERFORMANCE
Stage
Sound tent
HOW UPSET AM I AT MISSING THE BANDS I MISSED?
REALLY upset!
What a relief!
Superchunk
Built to Spill
Cat Power
Dan Deacon
Man Man
Erase Errata
Disco Bisquits & Umphrey's McGee
SELECTED SHOWS IN DETAIL
Great
Okay
Bad
Duration of set
the Beastie Boys
Feist
Band of Horses
TV on the Radio
Sonic Youth
Ted Leo
WHAT WAS JOGGING THROUGH MY MIND AT THE SHOWS I WENT TO?
G H I J K L M N O P Q S T U V W Y Z
You know what? I'm having a great time!
Grumpy as I may or may not be, it's good to be here.
This rain is kind of a drag, but sorta nice in a way.
Was Superchunk any good when they played?
Gotta say... this crowd looks bored to death.
There is a ton of facial hair going on.
Grown men LOVE beach balls.
Packed like a sardine in a tin can... BOO.
Dodgeball as a spectator sport? Ummm...
More like a singles swap.
If I'm not at home watching "Law & Order" re-runs do they actually exist? [Homesick.]
It's really hard to watch some people flopping around in bathing suits.
WHY PEOPLE CAME TO THE POOL
Free Shows
To party
To see the band
Pay Shows
To party
To see the band
ACTIVITY PARTICIPATION
Slip 'n Slide
Grown men
Women + children
Dodgeball
Grown men
Women + children
SPONSOR LOGOS DISPLAYED AT TWO SHOWS
350
325
300
275
250
225
200
175
150
125
100
75
50
25
0
G
T
Cell Phone
Beer
Energy Drink
ENDURING THE LENGTH OF LINES
Step right up!
Ghostland Observatory merch
Ponderosa Stop... Beer, Food and Entrance
V.I.P. desk at TV on the Radio
Feist pierogi stand
The Beastie Boys ice cream.
Band of Horses beer
The Beastie Boys beer
Blonde Redhead entrance
We're gonna be here 'til next summer!
MY SUMMER MOOD SWINGS
Stoked
Bummed
Duration of the pool schedule
Keep the shows coming!
I think I've spent too much time here and not a pool with water in it.
THE POOL SHOWS BY THE NUMBERS
Public Porta-Potties
Times I wished I wasn't there.
Baby with giant ear muff sighting!
Times I ate watermelon.
Times I wished I knew someone at the show.
Times I wished I didn't know anyone at the show.
New condos under contruction within view.
Times I actually thought the merch table had nice stuff.
Christopher Walken T-Shirts that said; "I HAVE A FEVER."
Wind-chimes on the headstocks of guitars [TV on the Radio].
Costume changes [Erasure].
T-shirts that said: "GOD IS A DJ."
CLOSING THOUGHTS: PYRAMIDS OF HIGHS AND LOWS
The space itself.
The free-ness of the free Sunday shows.
Erasure's stage set: huge rotating diamonds and a purple flight of stairs!?
Erasure's stage set [same reason].
The cost of the pay-shows. [i.e. The Beastie Boys = $49]
The fact that this was probably the last summer of music at the pool.
Au revoir pool shows! [Hello fall!]

I like linear charts quite a bit, because they enable you to discuss two things at the same time. You might like some parts of a show but hate others, and a linear chart can express both of these things in one simple illustration. It's like the music itself—there's a beginning and an end and a lot of things happen in between that contradict each other. I really enjoy that idea. Here's a chart of two shows by the Boredoms. [64] One concert was significantly shorter than the other. I was thinking about food the whole time and about Joba Chamberlain maybe converting to a starter for the Yankees, because the Boredoms are actually a slightly boring band.

Laughs

The next chart illustrates Usher's new song featuring Young Jeezy, which is amazing, "Second-by-Second." [65] As you can see, I've plotted the production of the song against the rapping and singing.

A while back, Vampire Weekend, who I love to death, and The New Pornographers, who I hate to death, played together at the Bowery Ballroom and I made this chart. [66] The guy from the New Pornographers came off like the most arrogant guy ever. I know he's probably a good dude, but the banter was awkward.

Laughs

[64] "The Boredoms at Terminal 5 and Other Music," *New York Times*, 2008, Andrew Kuo

THE BOREDOMS AT TERMINAL 5 AND OTHER MUSIC

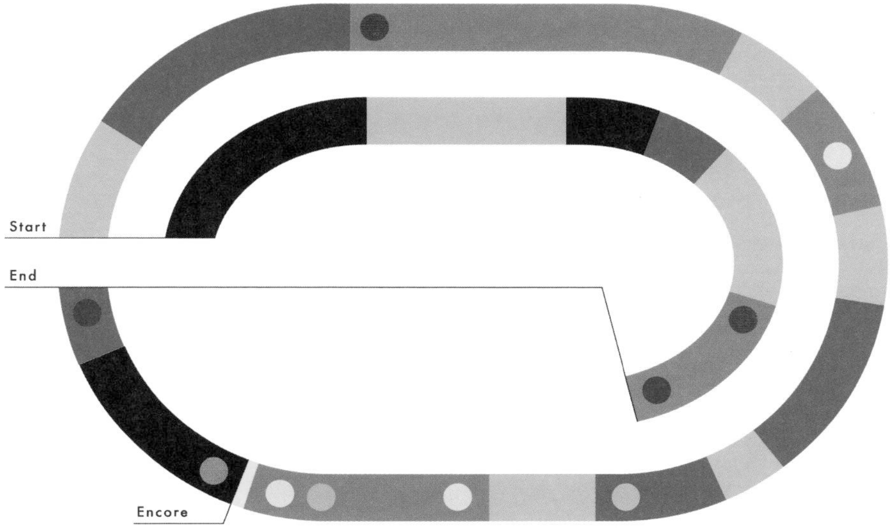

Start

End

Encore

Terminal 5

Other Music

Who needs drugs when you've got this!? Someone get my bongo!

It's tough to wipe the grin off my face... Keep going! Get louder! More everything!

As someone dutifully reminded me, "This is still better than most things."

It's like eating a bowl of oatmeal... every bite is the same texture.

Honestly? This is a few degrees away from a Santana show [in the bad way].

THINGS THAT I WAS THINKING ABOUT OTHER THAN THE SHOW

Tacos.

Joba Chamberlain needs to stay in the bullpen.

Is marijuana as fun as everyone says it is?

It's ridulous that you cannot get an amazing taco for under $2 downtown.

I wonder if "drum circle" translates to japanese.

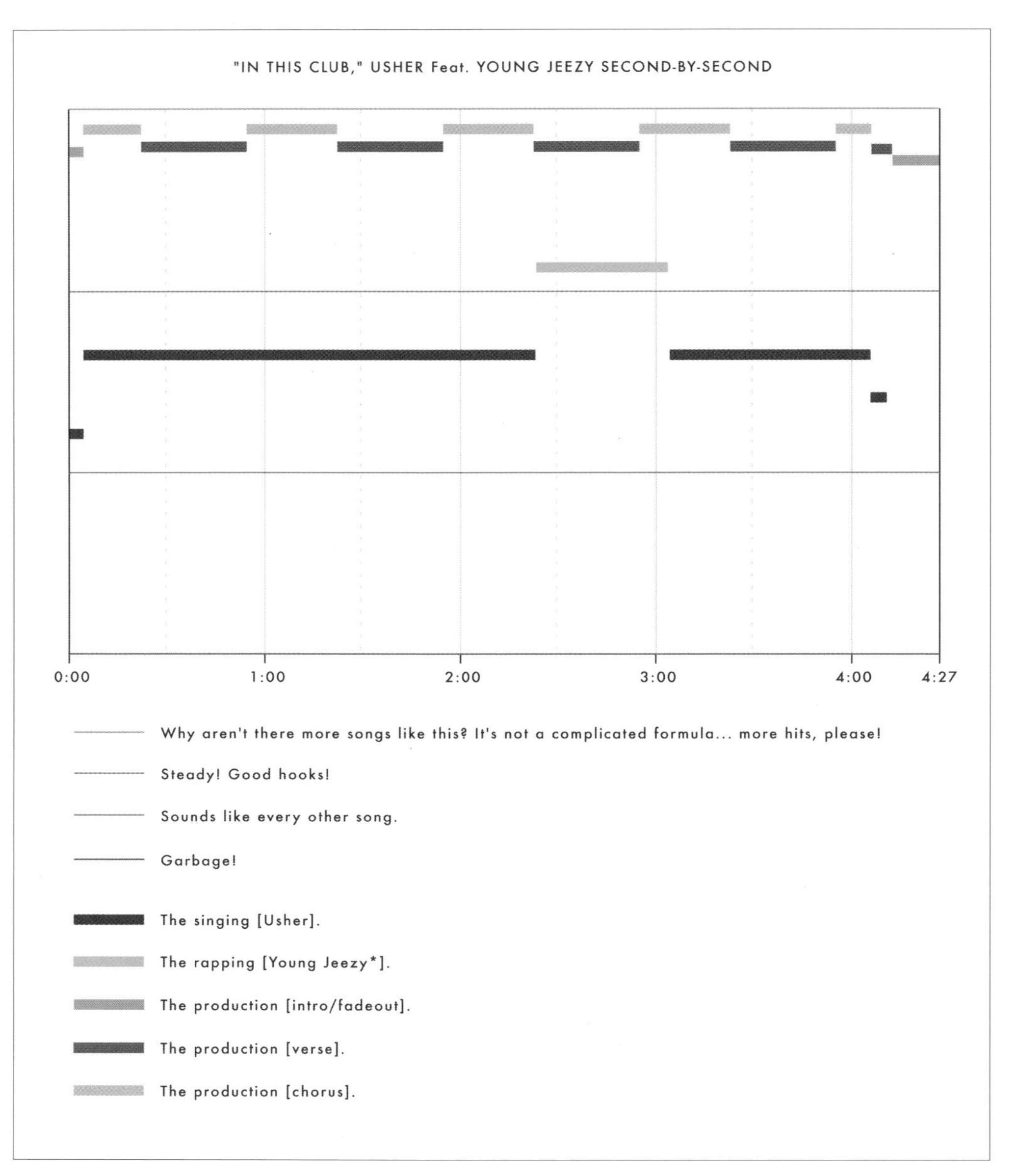

[65]

[65] "'In This Club,' Usher Feat. Young Jeezy Second-by-Second," *New York Times*, 2008, Andrew Kuo

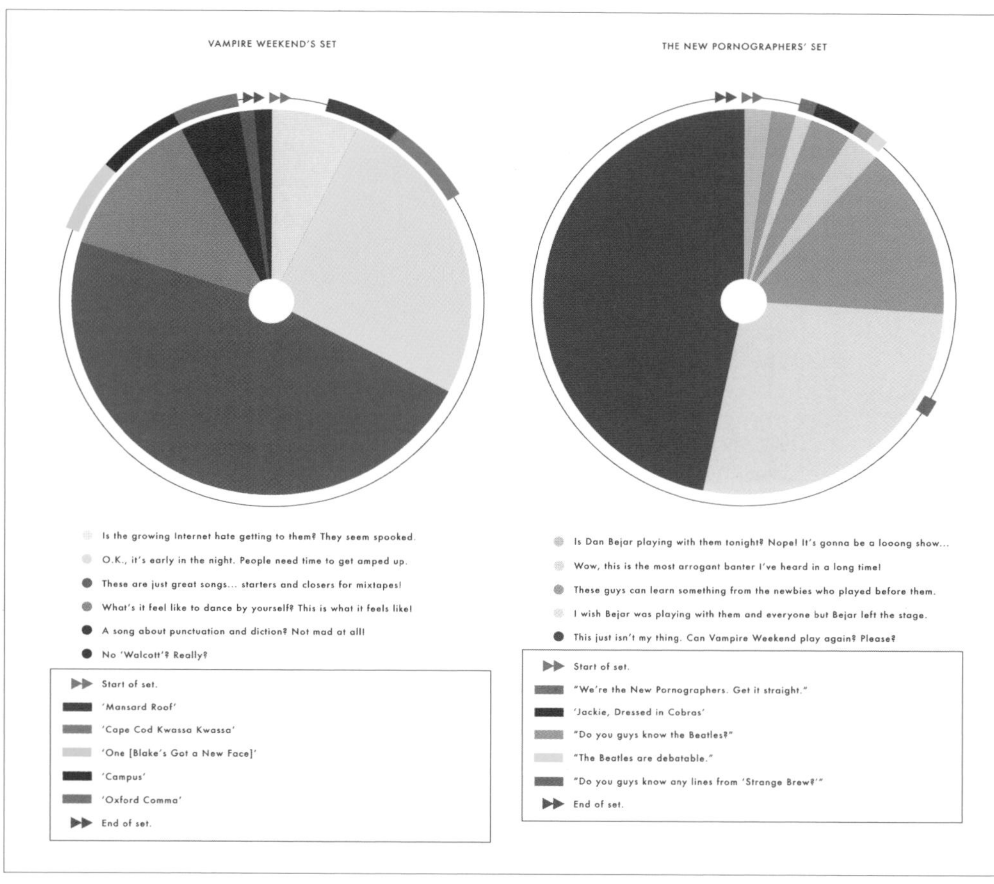
VAMPIRE WEEKEND'S SET
THE NEW PORNOGRAPHERS' SET
Is the growing Internet hate getting to them? They seem spooked.
O.K., it's early in the night. People need time to get amped up.
These are just great songs... starters and closers for mixtapes!
What's it feel like to dance by yourself? This is what it feels like!
A song about punctuation and diction? Not mad at all!
No 'Walcott'? Really?
Start of set.
'Mansard Roof'
'Cape Cod Kwassa Kwassa'
'One [Blake's Got a New Face]'
'Campus'
'Oxford Comma'
End of set.
Is Dan Bejar playing with them tonight? Nope! It's gonna be a looong show...
Wow, this is the most arrogant banter I've heard in a long time!
These guys can learn something from the newbies who played before them.
I wish Bejar was playing with them and everyone but Bejar left the stage.
This just isn't my thing. Can Vampire Weekend play again? Please?
Start of set.
"We're the New Pornographers. Get it straight."
'Jackie, Dressed in Cobras'
"Do you guys know the Beatles?"
"The Beatles are debatable."
"Do you guys know any lines from 'Strange Brew?'"
End of set.

[66] "Vampire Weekend's Set and The New Pornographers' Set," *New York Times*, 2007, Andrew Kuo

The Siren Music Festival chart is really hard to read. [67] I was even confused when I finished it.

Laughs

Laughs

Recently, I've started reviewing reviews. Here's the original review of a Foals show [68], and this is what I did to it. [69] Now you can just read it at a glance. I've also been reviewing incoming text messages. My friend the Jammer was at a Battles show that I missed and sent me a message that read "dork vortex," so I charted my reaction to her text. My friend Geico Man sent me a text message from a Vampire Weekend concert in Seattle and I liked that. It made me happy. [70]

Next up is a diagram of a Black Mountain show that I didn't like at all. [71] I made a chart that reminds me of Superman III or II when the aliens came in on these panes of glass.

The Fader magazine asked me to do a chart about my history of music, so I took key music bands and musicians and created these weird intersecting ellipses. [72] The diagram was based on the idea that this was a musical "universe" that intersects and crosses over each other a lot. If you stare at it long enough, it kind of works.

[67] "The Siren Festival: Actual and Hypothetical," *New York Times*, 2007, Andrew Kuo [68] "A Band That Cradles Its Rock, Even Under All Those Layers of Expectations," *New York Times*, 2008, Kelefa Sanneh. [69] "Review of Foals Review," www.earlboykins.blogspot.com, 2008, Andrew Kuo

[67]

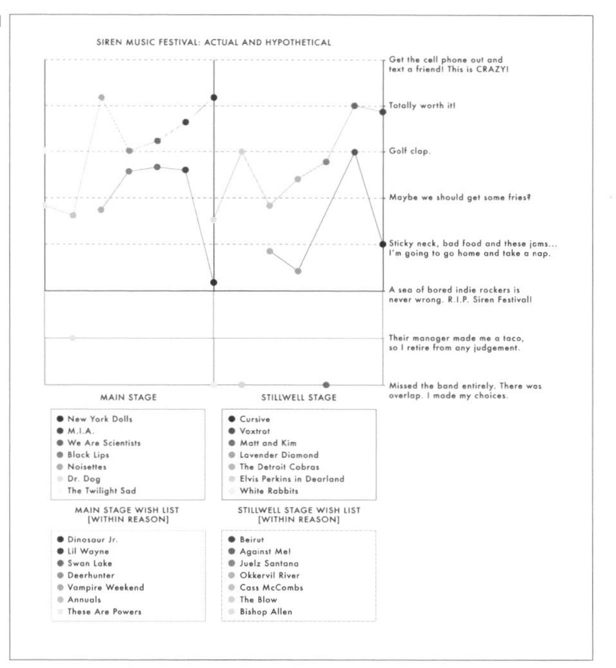

[68]

MUSIC REVIEW

A Band That Cradles Its Rock, Even Under All Those Layers of Expectations

Foals performing at the Bowery Ballroom on Tuesday night.

By KELEFA SANNEH
Published: February 14, 2008

SIGN IN TO E-MAIL OR SAVE THIS
PRINT
SHARE

Yannis Philippakis, lead singer of the emerging British band Foals, spent most of Tuesday night with both his hands on his chest. He wasn't being shy; he was playing the guitar. Like the bass player and the other guitarist, he wore a short strap, so the instrument was almost under his chin. And like them, he worked high on the fretboard, peeling off nimble riffs without ever uncrooking his arm.

The band had come to the Bowery Ballroom to play a short, tight set in support of an album that hasn't been released yet. "Antidotes," the debut Foals album, is scheduled to be out in Britain on March 24; Sub Pop plans to release the American version two weeks later. And on Tuesday night Mr. Philippakis seemed to enjoy the chance to play for a receptive audience full of curious listeners who had — as yet — no strong feelings about his band.

Suffice it to say that Foals inspires stronger feelings across the ocean, where it's possible for a band specializing in taut, knotty, danceable post-punk to be considered the next big thing. Foals appeared on a recent cover of the excitable music magazine NME, given pride of place on a list of "new bands that will define the year"; inside the keyboardist Edwin Congreave was quoted saying: "Hype is like a fever. It makes you feel ill." On the band's MySpace page there is a sarcastic and defensive self-description: "SNOTTY ART SCHOOL DROPOUTS HUNGRY FOR THE DOLLAR."

In America no band with a yelping singer and a jittery sound is likely to be considered money-hungry or definitive of 2008. Still, it's not hard to figure out why the Brits are so worked up. This music is rigorous enough and weird enough to separate Foals from the dance-punk explosion of a few years ago. Bands like Bloc Party and Battles are common reference points, but Foals also evokes — perhaps unintentionally — 1990s American post-hardcore bands like Clikatat Ikatowi and All Sears. Or maybe they just evoke that mythical, ever-recurring moment when young noisemakers hike up their guitar straps and start playing dance music.

During "Two Steps, Twice," a glimmering two-guitar ostinato set the scene as the precise rhythm section arrived, slow and heavy at first, then twice as fast. After a set punctuated by an unexpected outburst (apparently one of the musicians wasn't feeling well), the band members returned for an encore, with Mr. Philippakis gamely playing dumb.

"The people upstairs were like, 'It's tradition, you have to do it here,' " he said of the encore, as if he were describing an exotic ritual instead of a rock-club cliché. And with that, the band members jumped into "Mathletics," twitching in time to a disco-derived groove.

[69]

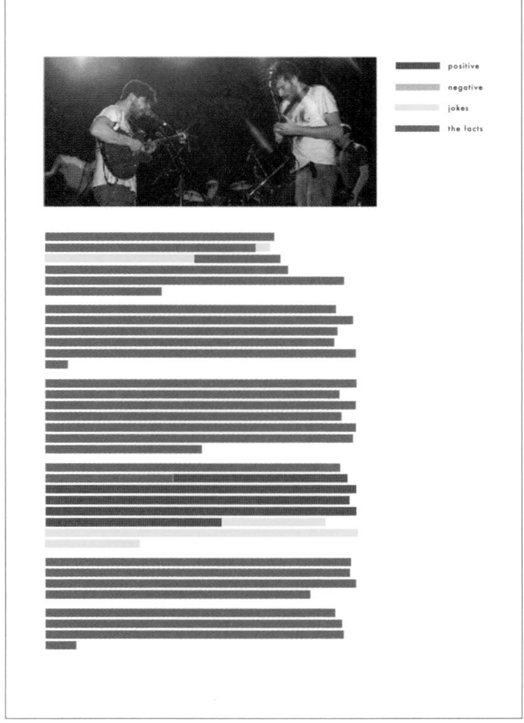

[70]

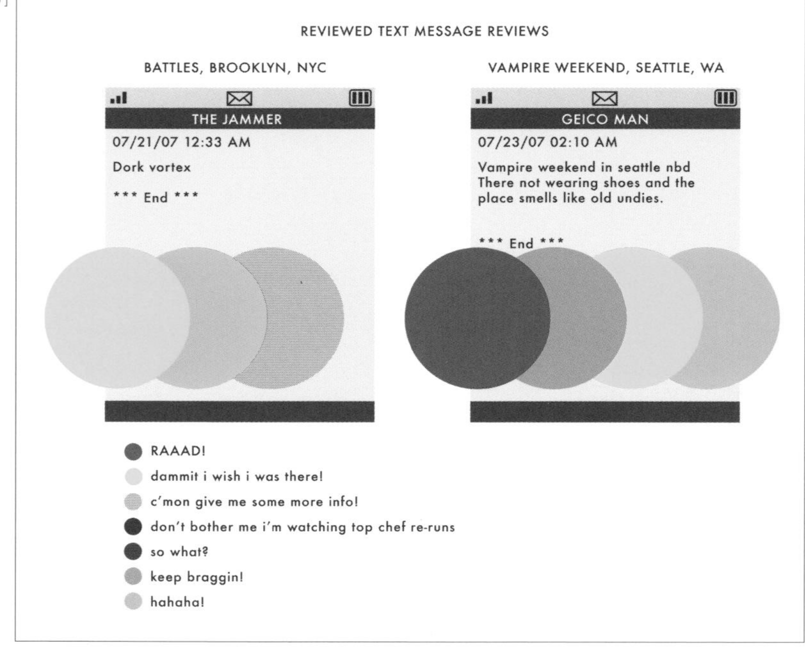

REVIEWED TEXT MESSAGE REVIEWS
BATTLES, BROOKLYN, NYC
THE JAMMER
07/21/07 12:33 AM
Dork vortex
*** End ***
VAMPIRE WEEKEND, SEATTLE, WA
GEICO MAN
07/23/07 02:10 AM
Vampire weekend in seattle nbd
There not wearing shoes and the
place smells like old undies.
*** End ***
RAAAD!
dammit i wish i was there!
c'mon give me some more info!
don't bother me i'm watching top chef re-runs
so what?
keep braggin!
hahaha!

[71]

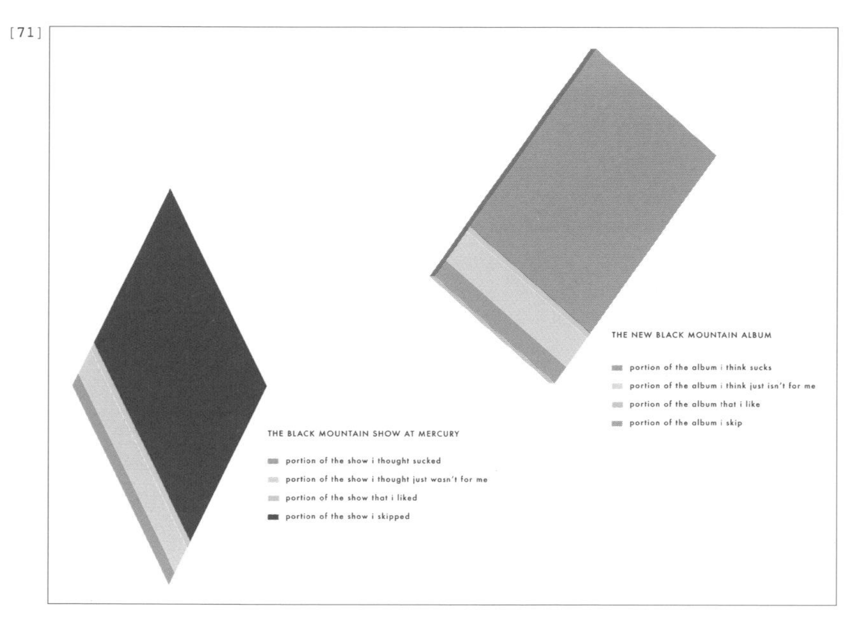

THE NEW BLACK MOUNTAIN ALBUM
portion of the album i think sucks
portion of the album i think just isn't for me
portion of the album that i like
portion of the album i skip
THE BLACK MOUNTAIN SHOW AT MERCURY
portion of the show i thought sucked
portion of the show i thought just wasn't for me
portion of the show that i liked
portion of the show i skipped

[70] "Reviewed Text Message Reviews," www.earlboykins.blogspot.com, 2008, Andrew Kuo [71] "The Black Mountain Show at Mercury/The New Black Mountain Album," www.earlboykins.blogspot.com, 2008, Andrew Kuo

[72]

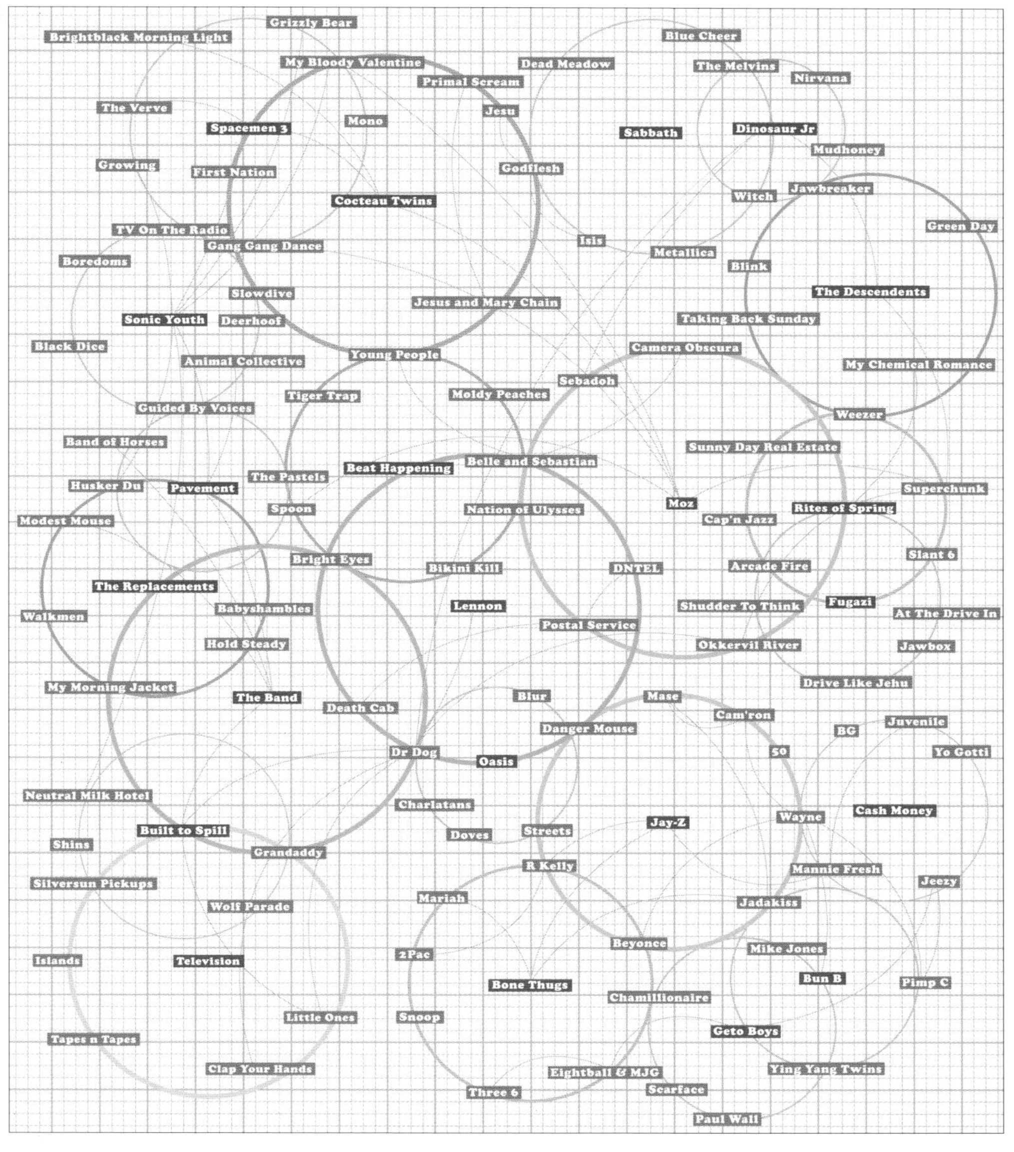

[72] "The History of Music," *The Fader*, 2007, Andrew Kuo

And here is a review of Panda Bear. [73] I thought it was very informative.

The Black Dice poster [74] might be the ugliest thing I've ever made; it is a visual reduction of the Beach Boys' *Pet Sounds* record; the white spot represents the goat they're petting. If you know the record, you know what I'm talking about. Even though the poster is ugly, I like the concept behind it, because it reminds me of what John was saying earlier about stripping everything down and making it simple. I think that's a very liberating feeling.

Laughs

[73] "Panda Bear Review Review," www.earlboykins.blogspot.com, 2007, Andrew Kuo [74] "Black Dice Poster," 2007, Andrew Kuo

[73]

[74]

A little while ago, I made a video with my friend Sneezy for Animal Collective's single, "Water Curses." [75] I knew that the video would mostly be watched on YouTube, so I wanted to make something that felt like it belonged on YouTube in terms of color, resolution, and concept. Even if you project it in high definition on a big screen, the video will still look like it was on YouTube. The pixilated screen grab you see here is Roy Orbison. The video itself is based off of the Traveling Wilburys' video, "Handle with Care." I like the sentiment of both the Animal Collective and Traveling Wilburys' songs playing off each other.

Another thing I've been playing around with lately is to create faces out of charts—crooked-mouth faces as I call them. A lot of them describe how I relate to things. This one, for example, is about music in my life. [76] And this one shows my relationship to art. [77] As you can see, I was inspired by the artist Sophie Calle, whose work I really love. Here you see the two charts hanging in my studio. [78] This is what I look at every day.

Laughs

I also made a chart of me getting drunk and my regrets. [79] And what happens when you're around me when I get drunk. I start off really grumpy. Then I kind of get happy, and then I get really happy, and after that I regret everything that I do.

Laughs

[75] "Animal Collective 'Water Curses' Video," 2008, director: Andrew Kuo; animator: Snejina Latev [76] "My Relationship to the Music as of May 8, 2008 (Missing-Tooth Face)," 2008, Andrew Kuo

[75]

[76]

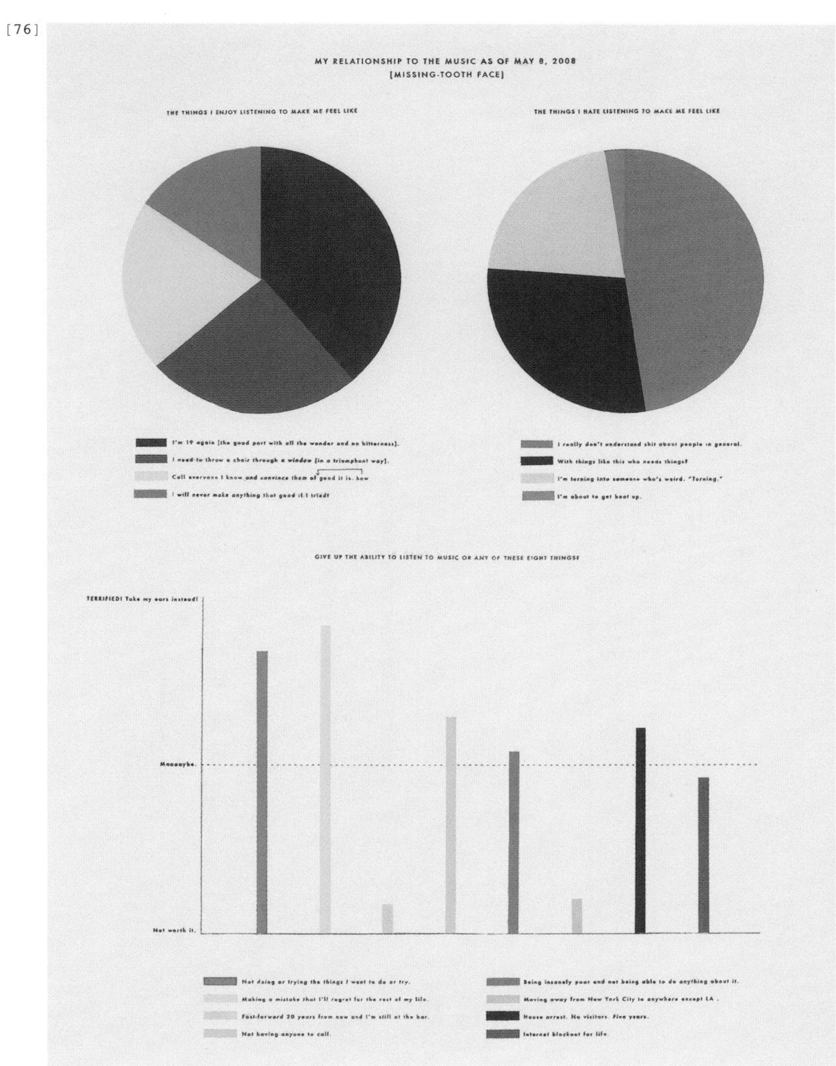
MY RELATIONSHIP TO THE MUSIC AS OF MAY 8, 2008
[MISSING-TOOTH FACE]
THE THINGS I ENJOY LISTENING TO MAKE ME FEEL LIKE
THE THINGS I HATE LISTENING TO MAKE ME FEEL LIKE
I'm 19 again [the good part with all the wonder and no bitterness].
I need to throw a chair through a window [in a triumphant way].
Call everyone I know and convince them of good it is. how
I will never make anything that good if I tried!
I really don't understand shit about people in general.
With things like this who needs things?
I'm turning into someone who's weird. "Turning."
I'm about to get beat up.
GIVE UP THE ABILITY TO LISTEN TO MUSIC OR ANY OF THESE EIGHT THINGS?
TERRIFIED! Take my ears instead!
Maaaaybe.
Not worth it.
Not doing or trying the things I want to do or try.
Making a mistake that I'll regret for the rest of my life.
Fast-forward 20 years from now and I'm still at the bar.
Not having anyone to call.
Being insanely poor and not being able to do anything about it.
Moving away from New York City to anywhere except LA .
House arrest. No visitors. Five years.
Internet blackout for life.

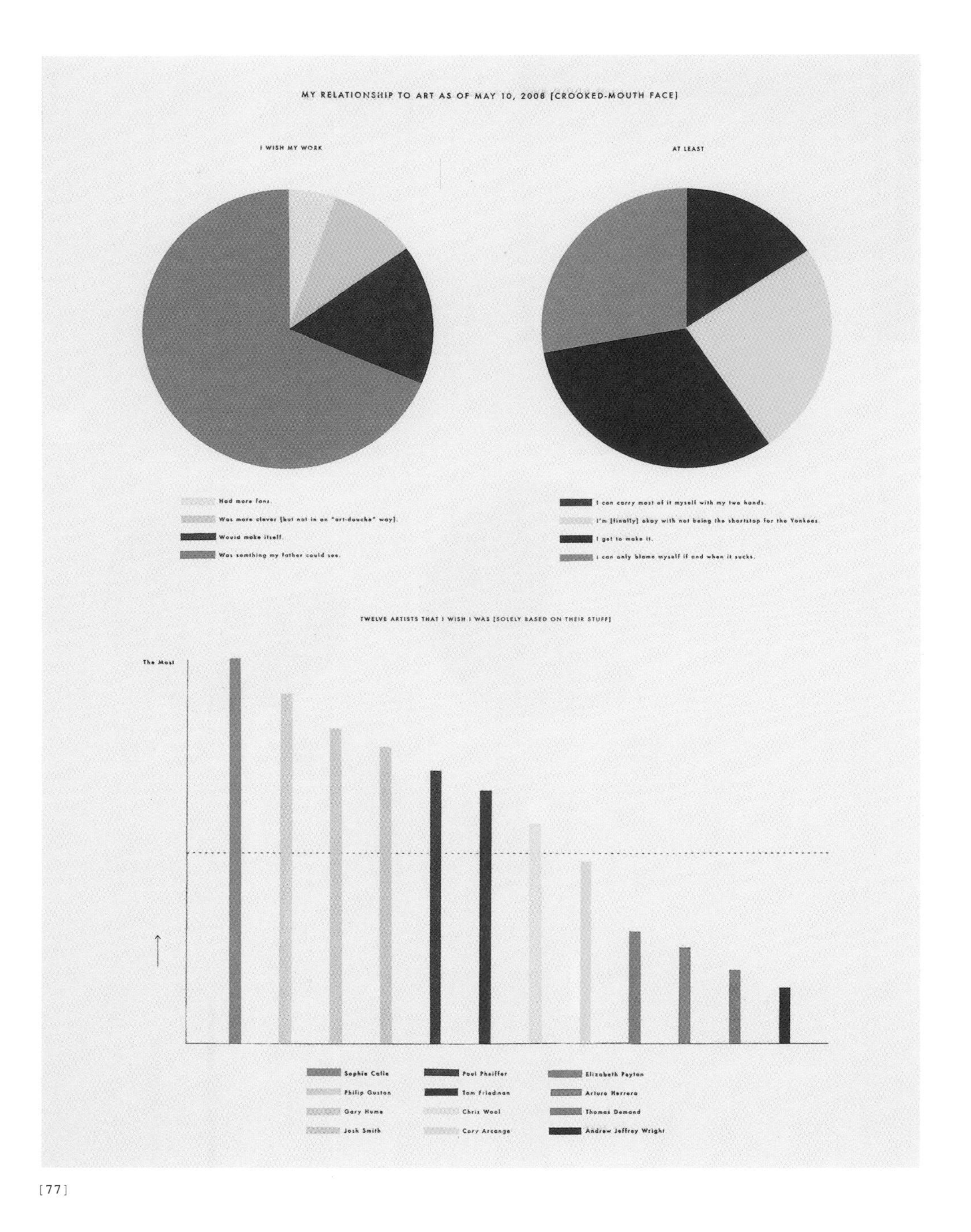
MY RELATIONSHIP TO ART AS OF MAY 10, 2008 [CROOKED-MOUTH FACE]
I WISH MY WORK
AT LEAST
Had more fans.
Was more clever [but not in an "art-douche" way].
Would make itself.
Was somthing my father could see.
I can carry most of it myself with my two hands.
I'm [finally] okay with not being the shortstop for the Yankees.
I get to make it.
I can only blame myself if and when it sucks.
TWELVE ARTISTS THAT I WISH I WAS [SOLELY BASED ON THEIR STUFF]
The Most
Sophie Calle
Philip Guston
Gary Hume
Josh Smith
Paul Pheiffer
Tom Friedman
Chris Wool
Cory Arcange
Elizabeth Payton
Arturo Herrera
Thomas Demand
Andrew Jeffrey Wright

[77]

[77] "My Relationship to Art as of May 10, 2008 (Crooked-Mouth Face)," 2008, Andrew Kuo [78] "Studio," photo by Andrew Kuo [79] Drinking as of May 15, 2008 (Crying-Eyes Face)," 2008, Andrew Kuo

[78]

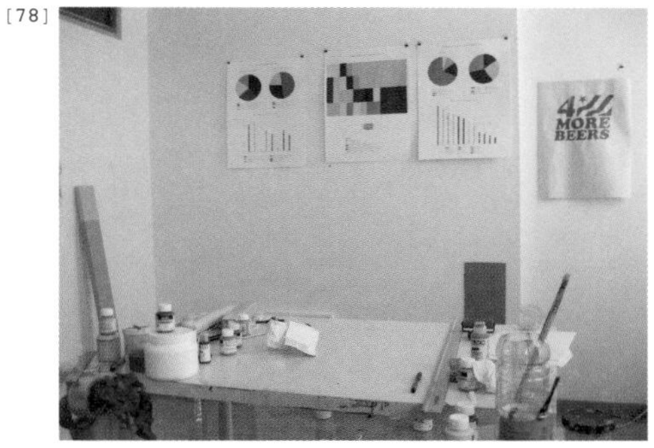
4 MORE BEERS

[79]

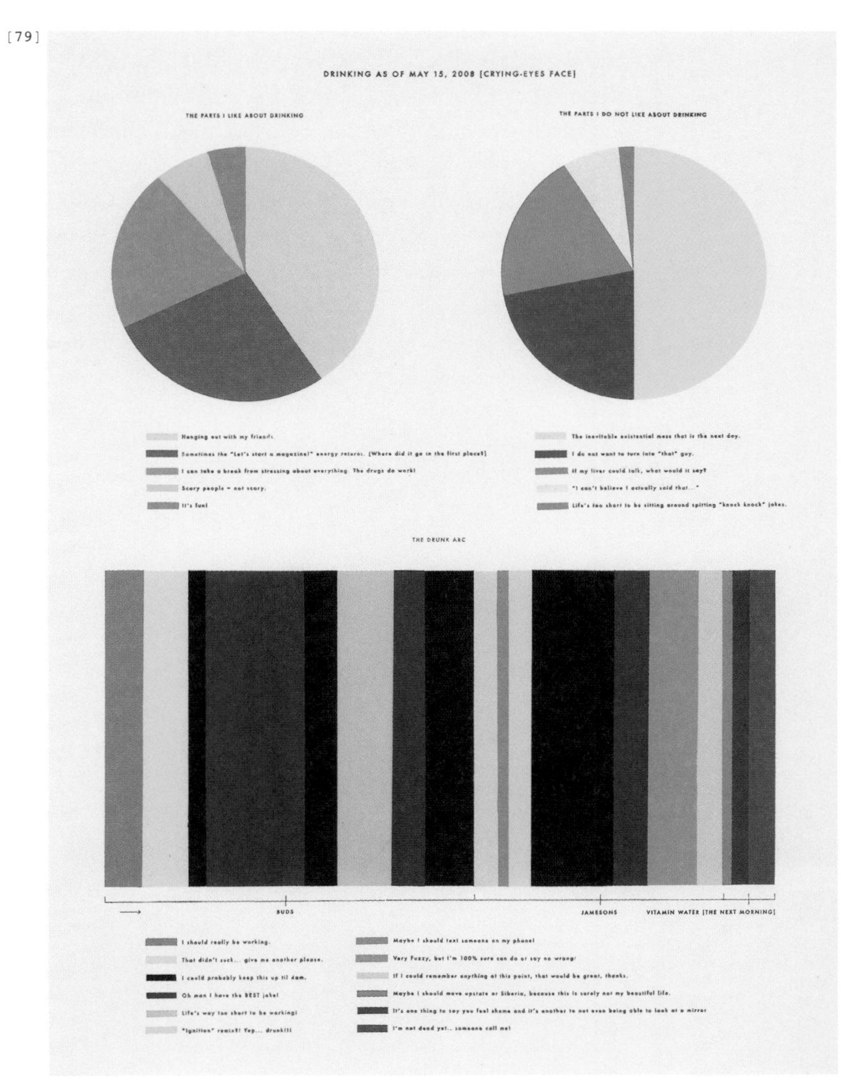
DRINKING AS OF MAY 15, 2008 [CRYING-EYES FACE]
THE PARTS I LIKE ABOUT DRINKING
THE PARTS I DO NOT LIKE ABOUT DRINKING
Hanging out with my friends.
Sometimes the "Let's start a magazine!" energy returns. [Where did it go in the first place?]
I can take a break from stressing about everything. The drugs do work!
Scary people = not scary.
It's fun!
The inevitable existential mess that is the next day.
I do not want to turn into "that" guy.
If my liver could talk, what would it say?
"I can't believe I actually said that..."
Life's too short to be sitting around spitting "knock knock" jokes.
THE DRUNK ARC
BUDS
JAMESONS
VITAMIN WATER [THE NEXT MORNING]
I should really be working.
That didn't suck... give me another please.
I could probably keep this up til 4am.
Oh man I have the BEST joke!
Life's way too short to be working!
"Ignition" remix?! Yep... drunk!!!
Maybe I should text someone on my phone!
Very Fuzzy, but I'm 100% sure can do or say no wrong!
If I could remember anything at this point, that would be great, thanks.
Maybe I should move upstate or Siberia, because this is surely not my beautiful life.
It's one thing to say you feel shame and it's another to not even being able to look at a mirror
I'm not dead yet.. someone call me!

On my ideal Tuesday [80], I drink lots of vitamin waters, stay at home, no one calls me, and I watch *Iron Chef* and *Hell's Kitchen*—such a great show.

Sometimes I also make sculptural diagrams, for example this piece that I called "How Much I Liked You Then and How Much I Like You Now." [81]

Laughs

I've had a number of exhibitions in New York, the last one closed this February. I showed some of my paper cutouts [83] as well as a couple of sculptures. [82] [84] [85] One of the sculptural diagrams was about my favorite bands. You can touch it, which to me was super exciting. I always felt that these things had more of a presence off the screen, away from the Internet. The physical part of it is really important to me, as I feel there's much more power there.

The other sculpture illustrated my fear of traveling. [85] I don't like to travel at all. I get really anxious. I'm afraid I'm going to be lonely, I'm afraid I'm going to miss my friends and my family, I'm afraid I'm going to die and no one will know, I'm afraid of losing my passport, I'm afraid of not eating good food—the whole scope. So I set the sculpted diagram up and then knocked it down. It was very poignant.

Laughs

[80] "My Ideal Slacker Tuesday (as of March 27, 2008)," 2008, Andrew Kuo
[81] "How Much I Liked You Then and How Much I Like You Now," 2008, Andrew Kuo

[80]

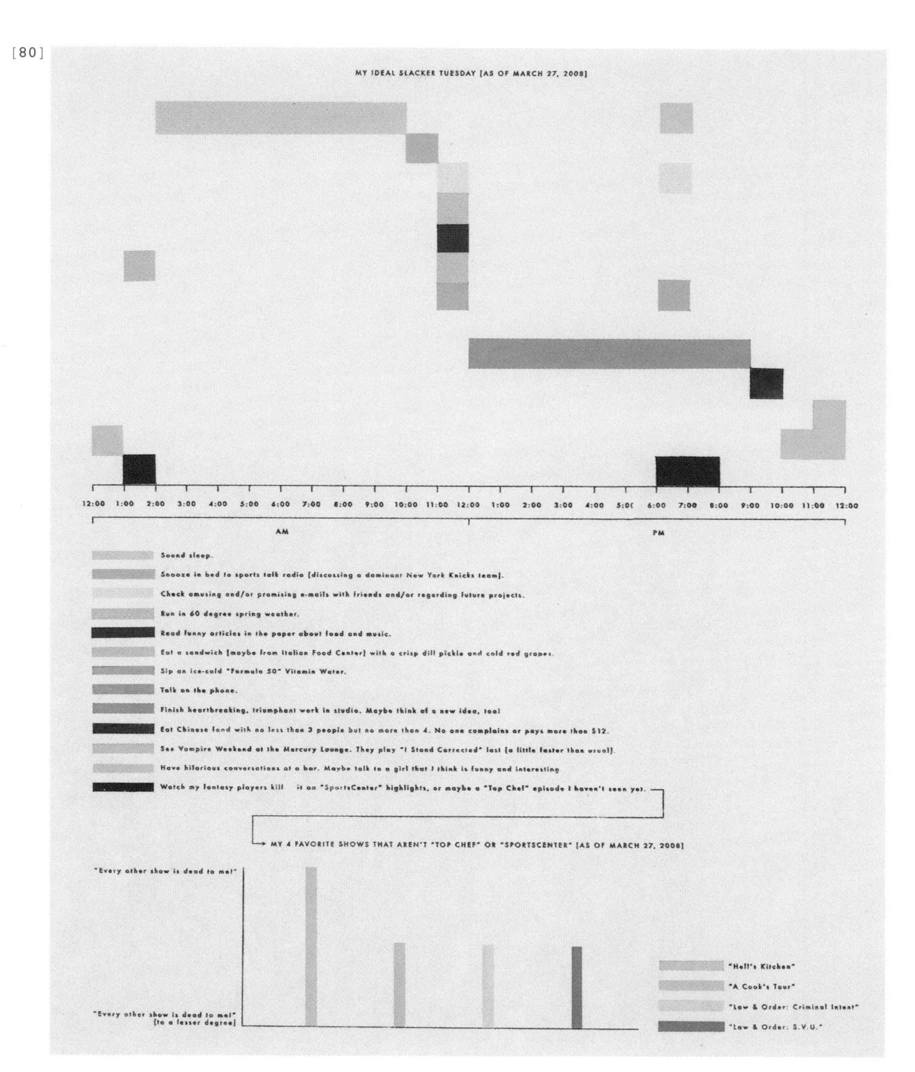
MY IDEAL SLACKER TUESDAY [AS OF MARCH 27, 2008]
12:00 1:00 2:00 3:00 4:00 5:00 6:00 7:00 8:00 9:00 10:00 11:00 12:00 1:00 2:00 3:00 4:00 5:0(6:00 7:00 8:00 9:00 10:00 11:00 12:00
AM
PM
Sound sleep.
Snooze in bed to sports talk radio [discussing a dominant New York Knicks team].
Check amusing and/or promising e-mails with friends and/or regarding future projects.
Run in 60 degree spring weather.
Read funny articles in the paper about food and music.
Eat a sandwich [maybe from Italian Food Center] with a crisp dill pickle and cold red grapes.
Sip an ice-cold "Formula 50" Vitamin Water.
Talk on the phone.
Finish heartbreaking, triumphant work in studio. Maybe think of a new idea, too!
Eat Chinese food with no less than 3 people but no more than 4. No one complains or pays more than $12.
See Vampire Weekend at the Mercury Lounge. They play "I Stand Corrected" last [a little faster than usual].
Have hilarious conversations at a bar. Maybe talk to a girl that I think is funny and interesting
Watch my fantasy players kill it on "SportsCenter" highlights, or maybe a "Top Chef" episode I haven't seen yet.
MY 4 FAVORITE SHOWS THAT AREN'T "TOP CHEF" OR "SPORTSCENTER" [AS OF MARCH 27, 2008]
"Every other show is dead to me!"
"Every other show is dead to me!" [to a lesser degree]
"Hell's Kitchen"
"A Cook's Tour"
"Law & Order: Criminal Intent"
"Law & Order: S.V.U."

[81]

[82]

[83]

[82] "Installation View of 'What Me Worry'," 2007
[83] "Cave," 2007, Andrew Kuo

[84]

[85]

[84] "Music Right Now," 2007, Andrew Kuo
[85] "What I Fear About Traveling," 2007, Andrew Kuo

Last November I charted the story of my life up to that point in time [86] [87] and recently I made a chart about everything that scares me. [88] [89]

And last, these are my favorite places in New York as of last year. [90]

Applause

MAEDA: **And now we have Fernanda Viégas. Welcome.**

[**86**] "My Life up until November 07," 2007, Andrew Kuo [**87**] "My Life up until November 07," 2007, Andrew Kuo [**88**] "Some Things I Am Scared of as of November 2007," 2007, Andrew Kuo [**89**] "Some Things I Am Scared of as of November 2007," 2007, Andrew Kuo [**90**] "My Favorite Places as of November 2007," 2007, Andrew Kuo

[86]

[87]

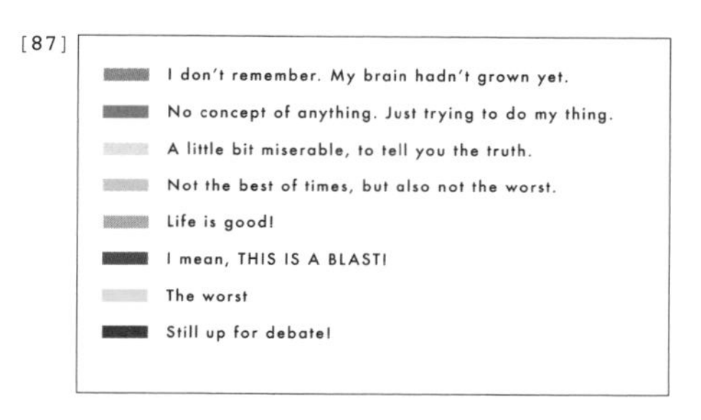

I don't remember. My brain hadn't grown yet.
No concept of anything. Just trying to do my thing.
A little bit miserable, to tell you the truth.
Not the best of times, but also not the worst.
Life is good!
I mean, THIS IS A BLAST!
The worst
Still up for debate!

[88]

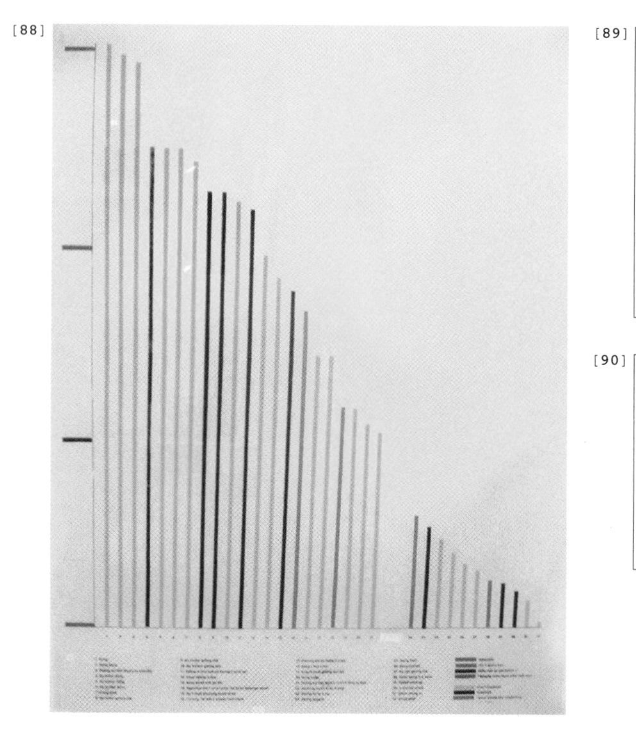

[89]

1. Dying.
2. Dying alone.
3. Finding out that there's no after-life.
4. My father dying.
5. My mother dying.
6. My brother dying.
7. Going blind.
8. My father getting sick.

[90]

A good chinese restaurant with friends.

My kitchen making pasta.

My couch watching a new Law & Order.

My studio just after deadlines.

At a Superchunk show. Alone is fine.

Enter Fernanda Viégas

VIÉGAS: Thank you. Before I talk about Many Eyes, the project that I'm working on right now, I thought I should take you back on a little bit of a time travel. Back in the 1990s, InfoViz—information visualization—used to be something that combined a lot of gaudy colors and lots of scientists looking at very complex data. InfoViz was something that used to be done by experts for experts. It was very serious stuff—it was your prototypical scientist trying to come up with some wonderful insights for science to communicate to the rest of the world. The field also used to be dominated by men.

I've been working with InfoViz for the last few years and noticed, however, that it has a lot of power when you take it out of the lab bubble, out of the academic bubble, and bring it to the rest of the world—when you have regular people looking at graphs and charts and even interacting with them. This insight has informed the work that I'm doing right now, together with a colleague of mine, Martin Wattenberg. Some of you might know him from the amazing information visualization pieces he's done.

What Martin and I started to realize is that when you make visualization accessible, people use it in many different ways. One of the things that visualization is good at is sparking conversation. People will look at graphs and want to talk about what they see. That inspired us to design Many Eyes, a space with interactive graphs and charts that gives people the opportunity to talk about them and to share them with each other.

Many Eyes is a website on which anyone can upload data, visualize data, and share these visualizations with others. If you see something interesting, you can point to things, you can ask questions, and someone can jump in and, hopefully, answer your question. It sort of looks like a media site. [91] At the top we feature a few visualizations, which we try to change every week. If you want to look at some of the latest, most recent visualizations that people have created on the site, you can explore them in a similar way as you would look through YouTube videos. [92]

[91] Many Eyes home page, IBM Research, 2008, designer: Fernanda Viégas
[92] Many Eyes visualization browsing, IBM Research, 2008

[91]

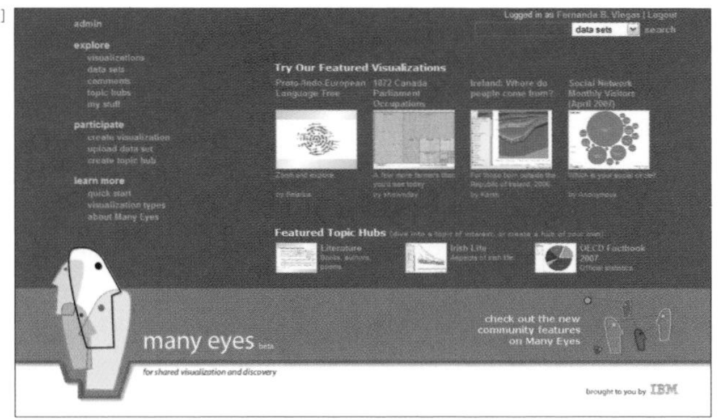
Logged in as Fernanda B. Viegas | Logout
data sets
search
admin
explore
participate
learn more
Try Our Featured Visualizations
Featured Topic Hubs
Literature
Irish Life
OECD Factbook 2007
check out the new community features on Many Eyes
many eyes
for shared visualization and discovery
brought to you by IBM

[92]

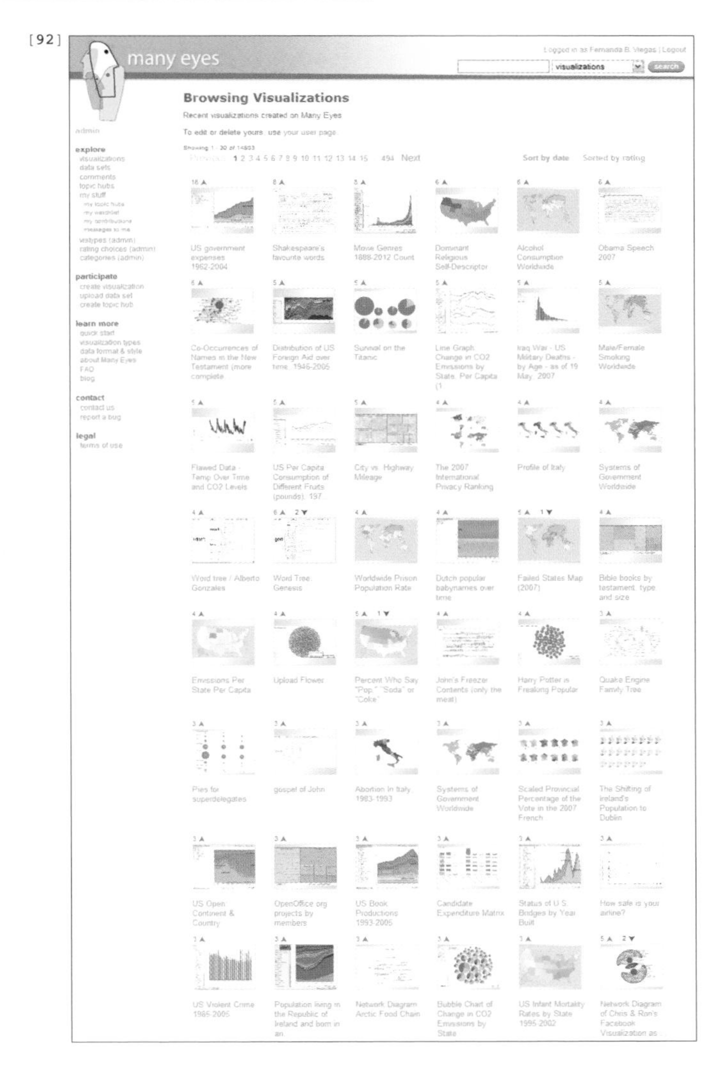
many eyes
Logged in as Fernanda B. Viegas | Logout
visualizations
search
Browsing Visualizations
Recent visualizations created on Many Eyes
To edit or delete yours, use your user page.
explore
participate
learn more
contact
legal
Sort by date
Sorted by rating

You get a sense of how diverse the different kinds of data are that people bring to the site and the different kinds of visualization techniques they're using, from maps to bar charts to more sophisticated things like the tree maps shown in the fourth row. The site was launched in January 2007, and so far people have created over fourteen thousand visualizations on Many Eyes, and we have lots of regular users.

So let me show you what one of these visualizations looks like. One of our users created this chart of U.S. government expenses since the 1960s. [93] It's basically a time series that shows how the U.S. government has been spending its budget by category, such as national defense, human resources, and so forth. The graph is interactive, so as I mouse over here, you can see, within human resources, this is social security, this is Medicare; within national defense, this is military personnel, procurement, and so forth. Then you can start playing with it. Right now we're looking at the chart in absolute numbers. But I might be interested in the percentages, so I can change absolute numbers to percentage and I can see human resources going way up and national defense, surprisingly, not going as much up as I would have expected. [94] The tree structure on the left of the graphic, which is similar to the folder structure you have on your computer, also tells you that the data set we're looking at is actually much bigger than what you can see here. This means you can explore, for instance, physical resources and just look at those. [95] You can drill down and look at natural resources, or at commerce, you name it. You can look at national defense and see that spending seems to be quite cyclical, depending on whether or not the country is at war.

[93][94][95] Many Eyes visualization of U.S. budget over time, IBM Research, 2008

[93]

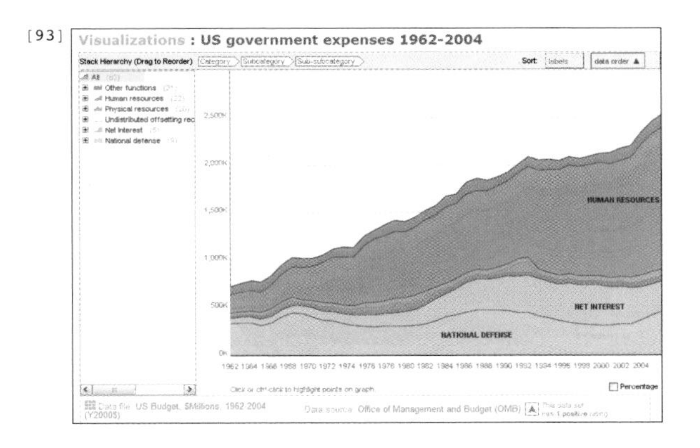
Visualizations : US government expenses 1962-2004
Stack Hierarchy (Drag to Reorder)
Category
Subcategory
Sub-subcategory
Sort:
labels
data order
All
Other functions
Human resources
Physical resources
Undistributed offsetting rec
Net interest
National defense
HUMAN RESOURCES
NET INTEREST
NATIONAL DEFENSE
2,500K
2,000K
1,500K
1,000K
500K
0K
1962 1964 1966 1968 1970 1972 1974 1976 1978 1980 1982 1984 1986 1988 1990 1992 1994 1996 1998 2000 2002 2004
Click or ctrl-click to highlight points on graph.
Percentage
Data file: US Budget, $Millions, 1962-2004 (Y2000$)
Data source: Office of Management and Budget (OMB)

[94]

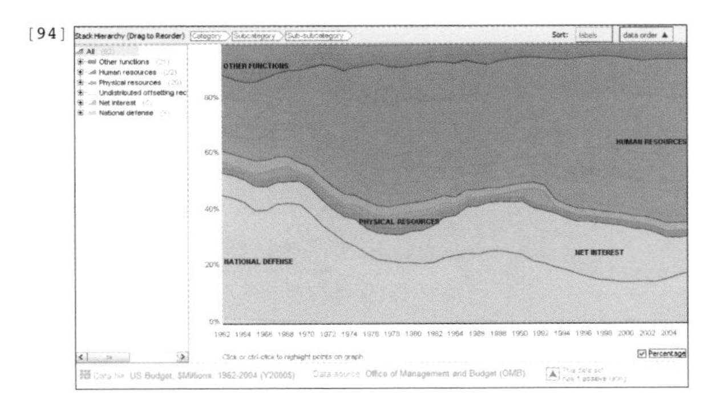
Stack Hierarchy (Drag to Reorder)
Category
Subcategory
Sub-subcategory
Sort:
labels
data order
All
Other functions
Human resources
Physical resources
Undistributed offsetting rec
Net interest
National defense
OTHER FUNCTIONS
HUMAN RESOURCES
PHYSICAL RESOURCES
NET INTEREST
NATIONAL DEFENSE
80%
60%
40%
20%
0%
1962 1964 1966 1968 1970 1972 1974 1976 1978 1980 1982 1984 1986 1988 1990 1992 1994 1996 1998 2000 2002 2004
Click or ctrl-click to highlight points on graph.
Percentage
Data file: US Budget, $Millions, 1962-2004 (Y2000$)
Data source: Office of Management and Budget (OMB)

[95]

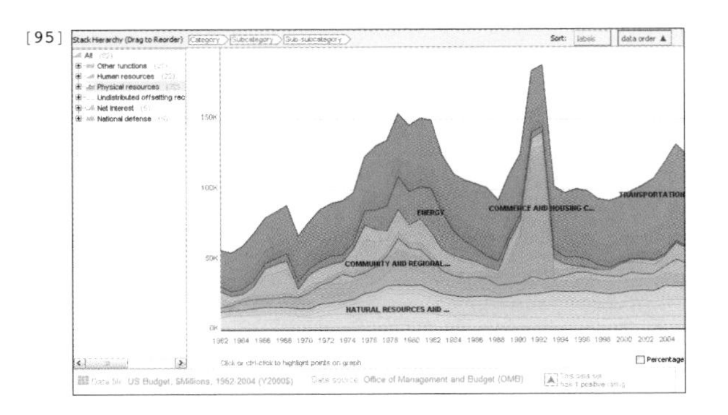
Stack Hierarchy (Drag to Reorder)
Category
Subcategory
Sub-subcategory
Sort:
labels
data order
All
Other functions
Human resources
Physical resources
Undistributed offsetting rec
Net interest
National defense
TRANSPORTATION
ENERGY
COMMERCE AND HOUSING C...
COMMUNITY AND REGIONAL ...
NATURAL RESOURCES AND ...
150K
100K
50K
0K
1962 1964 1966 1968 1970 1972 1974 1976 1978 1980 1982 1984 1986 1988 1990 1992 1994 1996 1998 2000 2002 2004
Click or ctrl-click to highlight points on graph.
Percentage
Data file: US Budget, $Millions, 1962-2004 (Y2000$)
Data source: Office of Management and Budget (OMB)

Every visualization on Many Eyes is also an opportunity to have a discussion with others. If I scroll down on this page, I can see that people have been leaving a lot of comments about what they see on this visualization. [96] It's like a regular blog: if you want to leave your own comment, you can enter it at the bottom of the page.

Next to some of the comments you can see small thumbnail images, which are a great feature of the site. One user left a comment saying, "What is this spike in commerce and housing credit?" He is talking about a specific peak within the graph. [97] When you click on the thumbnail next to his comment, it refreshes the page and takes you to the exact view that he is talking about. This is, of course, really important, because if someone is trying to show you something in an interactive visualization, you need to know what exact view he's talking about, because an interactive visualization can work a thousand different ways.

[96] Many Eyes visualization with user comments, IBM Research, 2008
[97] Many Eyes visualization of spike caused by the savings and loan bailout crisis, IBM Research, 2008

[96]

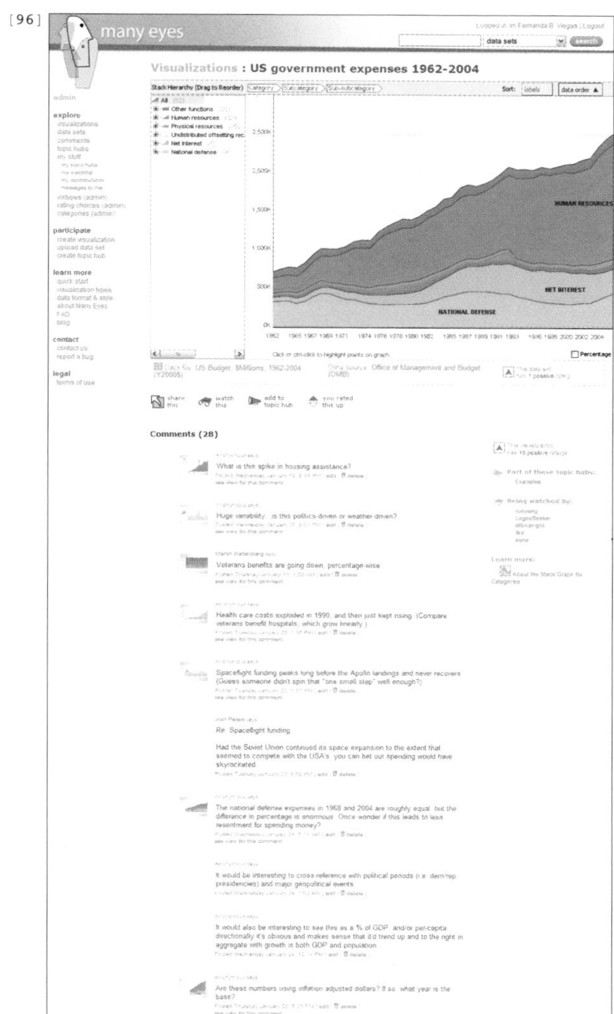

many eyes
data sets
search
Visualizations : US government expenses 1962-2004
Stack Hierarchy (Drag to Reorder)
Category
Subcategory
Sub-subcategory
Sort:
labels
data order
All
Other functions
Human resources
Physical resources
Undistributed offsetting rec
Net Interest
National defense
explore
participate
learn more
contact
legal
2,500K
2,000K
1,500K
1,000K
500K
0K
HUMAN RESOURCES
NET INTEREST
NATIONAL DEFENSE
Click or ctrl-click to highlight points on graph
Percentage
US Budget, $Millions, 1962-2004 (Y2000$)
Office of Management and Budget (OMB)
share this
watch this
add to topic hub
you rated this up
Comments (28)
What is this spike in housing assistance?
Huge variability ...is this politics-driven or weather-driven?
Veterans benefits are going down, percentage-wise
Health care costs exploded in 1990, and then just kept rising. (Compare veterans benefit hospitals, which grow linearly.)
Spaceflight funding peaks long before the Apollo landings and never recovers. (Guess someone didn't spin that "one small step" well enough?)
Re: Spaceflight funding
Had the Soviet Union continued its space expansion to the extent that seemed to compete with the USA's, you can bet our spending would have skyrocketed.
The national defense expenses in 1968 and 2004 are roughly equal, but the difference in percentage is enormous. Once wonder if this leads to less resentment for spending money?
It would be interesting to cross-reference with political periods (i.e. dem/rep presidencies) and major geopolitical events.
It would also be interesting to see this as a % of GDP, and/or per-capita directionally it's obvious and makes sense that it'd trend up and to the right in aggregate with growth in both GDP and population.
Are these numbers using inflation adjusted dollars? If so, what year is the base?

[97]

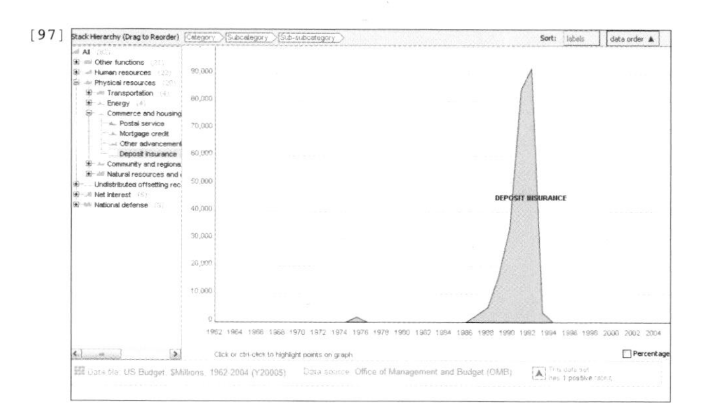

Stack Hierarchy (Drag to Reorder)
Category
Subcategory
Sub-subcategory
Sort:
labels
data order
All
Other functions
Human resources
Physical resources
Transportation
Energy
Commerce and housing
Postal service
Mortgage credit
Other advancement
Deposit insurance
Community and regiona
Natural resources and
Undistributed offsetting rec
Net Interest
National defense
90,000
80,000
70,000
60,000
50,000
40,000
30,000
20,000
10,000
0
DEPOSIT INSURANCE
1962 1964 1966 1968 1970 1972 1974 1976 1978 1980 1982 1984 1986 1988 1990 1992 1994 1996 1998 2000 2002 2004
Click or ctrl-click to highlight points on graph
Percentage
US Budget, $Millions, 1962-2004 (Y2000$)
Office of Management and Budget (OMB)

In this case, the user was looking at deposit insurance, which had a huge peak in the late 1980s/early 1990s due to the savings and loan bailout crisis. As you can see on the page, someone else came along and explained that this was what caused the amplitude. [98] So on Many Eyes people can point to trends and ask questions based on data visualizations. Every graphic on the site is linked to its data set [99], so you can see the raw numbers right away, if you want to. You can even copy the graphs, take them out of the site, to your Excel spreadsheet, and visualize them again.

We saw a lot of activity on the site as soon as we launched it. One of the things that was interesting to us was the kind of data people were bringing to the site. We offered all these techniques for visualizing numerical data, but we saw people trying to upload a lot of text on the site. They wanted to visualize things like their blog posts or entire books. They wanted to visualize the speeches of political candidates. So how do you do that?

In response to that question, we decided to create a few visualization techniques only for text. What I'm showing you here is called a word tree. [100] It's a way to visualize a whole bunch of text. This graph illustrates the testimony of Alberto Gonzales in 2007 about his role in the dismissal of U.S. attorneys. The cool thing about this visualization is that I don't even have to explain to you what's going on. You get it right away. Basically, the word tree is collapsing all parts of the text that repeat themselves.

[**98**] User comment on Many Eyes, IBM Research, 2008 [**99**] Data set page on Many Eyes, IBM Research, 2008 [**100**] Word tree visualization of Alberto Gonzales's testimony, IBM Research, 2008

[98]

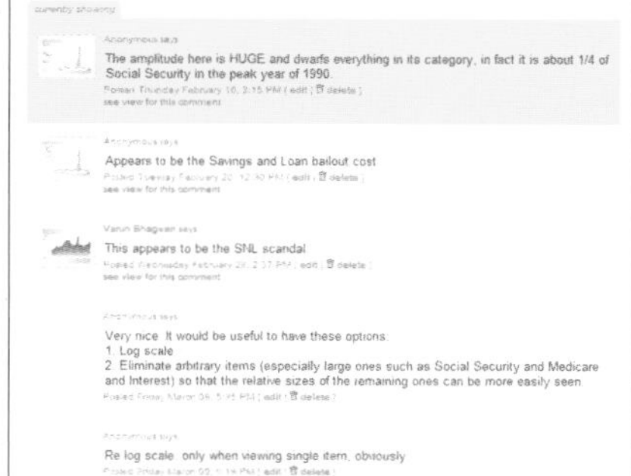

[99]

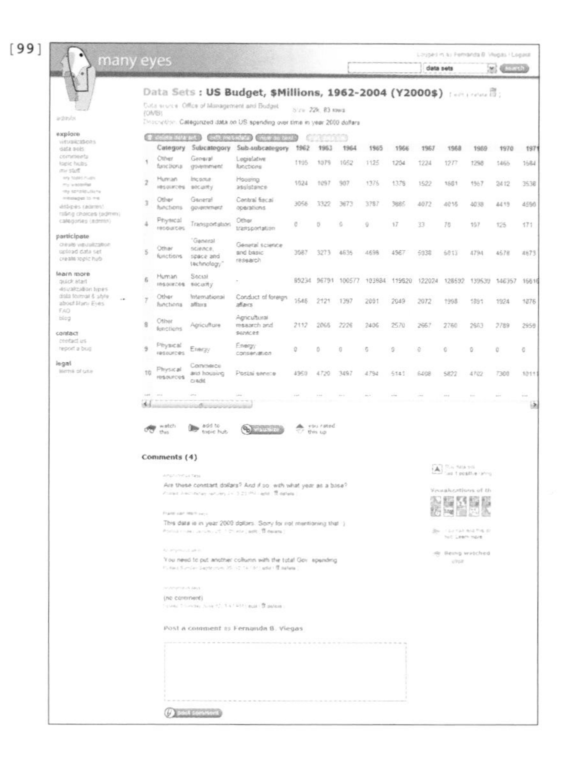

	Category	Subcategory	Sub-subcategory	1962	1963	1964	1965	1966	1967	1968	1969	1970	1971
1	Other functions	General government	Legislative functions	1105	1079	1052	1125	1204	1224	1277	1298	1466	1684
2	Human resources	Income security	Housing assistance	1024	1097	907	1376	1378	1522	1681	1967	2412	3538
3	Other functions	General government	Central fiscal operations	3056	3322	3673	3787	3885	4072	4016	4038	4419	4596
4	Physical resources	Transportation	Other transportation	0	0	0	9	17	33	70	107	125	171
5	Other functions	"General science, space and technology"	General science and basic research	3087	3273	4635	4698	4967	5938	6013	4794	4578	4673
6	Human resources	Social security	-	89234	96791	100577	103984	119820	122024	128592	139539	146357	15616
7	Other functions	International affairs	Conduct of foreign affairs	1546	2121	1397	2001	2049	2072	1998	1891	1924	1876
8	Other functions	Agriculture	Agricultural research and services	2112	2066	2226	2406	2570	2667	2760	2663	2789	2959
9	Physical resources	Energy	Energy conservation	0	0	0	0	0	0	0	0	0	0
10	Physical resources	Commerce and housing credit	Postal service	4959	4720	3497	4794	5141	6408	5822	4702	7300	1011
...	...	...	...	...	...	...	...	...	...	...	...	...	...

[100]

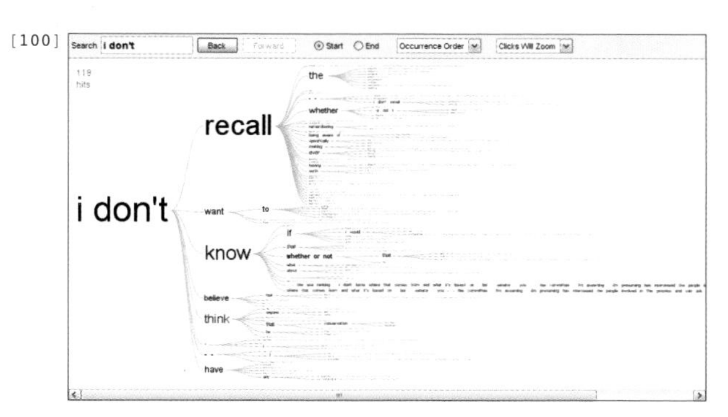

The user here searched for the words "I don't"—what are all the things that come after "I don't?" And the graph shows you that Gonzales said: "I don't recall, I don't know, I don't think, I don't believe." You can also start interacting with this result and ask, "What doesn't he recall?" [101] [102] [103] And he says, "I don't recall whether or not I made the decision that day." Let's go back and see what he doesn't know. "I don't know whether or not that puts everything behind us, quite frankly." Well, we don't know either. [104]

Laughs

Laughs

The tree allows you to do many different kinds of queries. For instance, you can put things at the end. If I want to know a ll the questions that were asked, I type in a question mark and put the question mark at the end. [105] This will show me all the questions that were asked during the testimony. As you can see, it can get very interesting to dive down and zoom in and zoom out, to play with things like text that you might not have thought about as being data. Usually, when we talk about data, we talk about numbers, but text is life, and it's a great opportunity for charts and graphs.

Many Eyes is a huge website, and I don't have time to show you everything, but the next few graphs give you a sense of the palette of visualization techniques that we provide, which range from very simple business graphs—things like bar charts and pie charts—to a lot more experimental things such as tree maps, social network diagrams, and so forth. [106]-[120]

[101]-[105] Word tree visualization of Alberto Gonzales's testimony, IBM Research, 2008

[101]

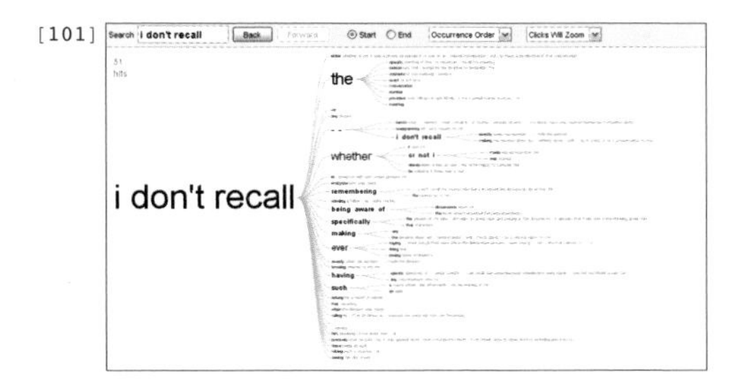

[102]

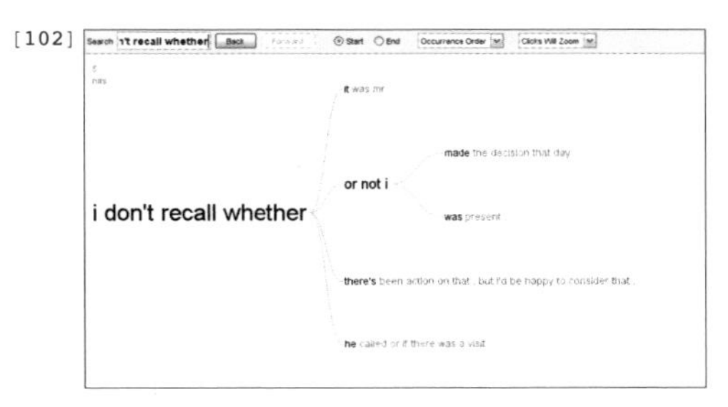

[103]

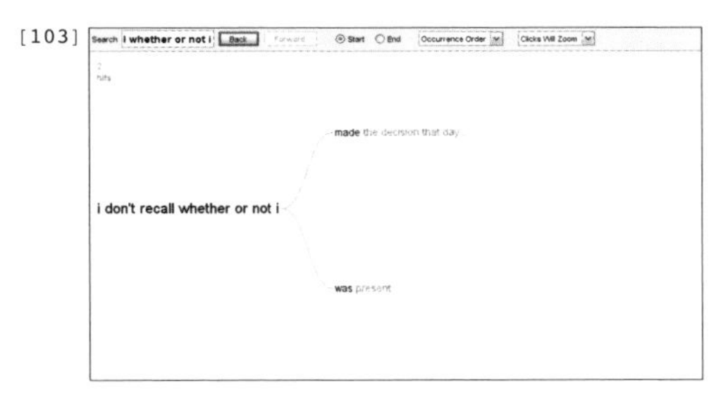

[104]

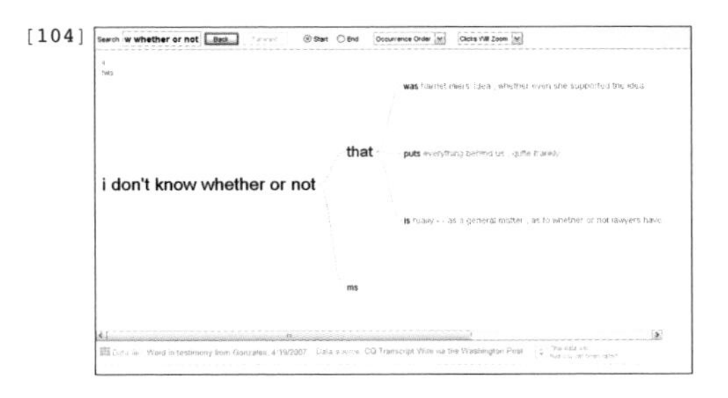

[105]

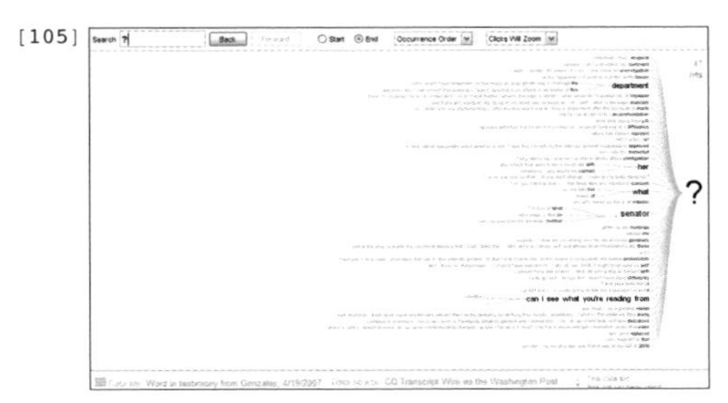

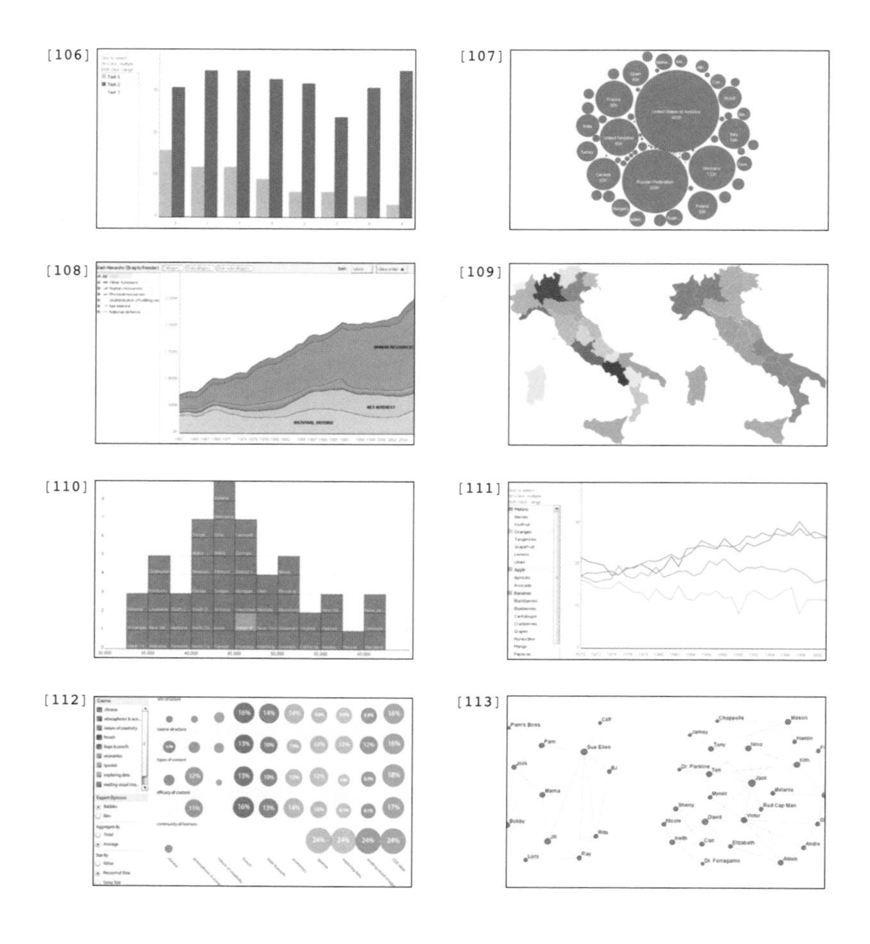

[106] Many Eyes, bar chart, IBM Research, 2008 [107] Many Eyes, bubble chart, IBM Research, 2008 [108] Many Eyes, stack graph with categories, IBM Research, 2008 [109] Many Eyes, country map, IBM Research, 2008 [110] Many Eyes, histogram, IBM Research, 2008 [111] Many Eyes, line graph, IBM Research, 2008 [112] Many Eyes, matrix chart, IBM Research, 2008 [113] Many Eyes, network diagram, IBM Research, 2008

[114]

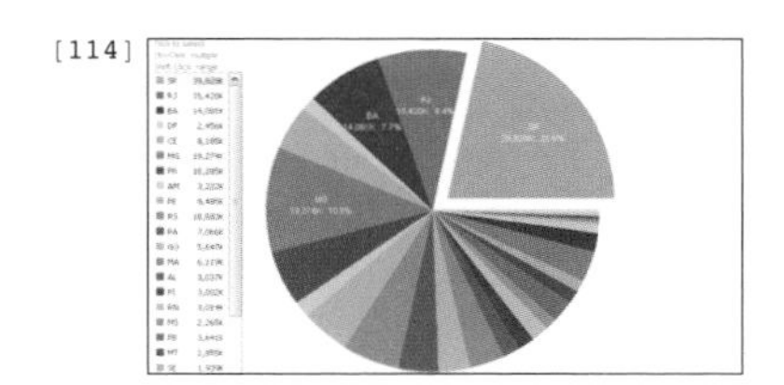

[115]

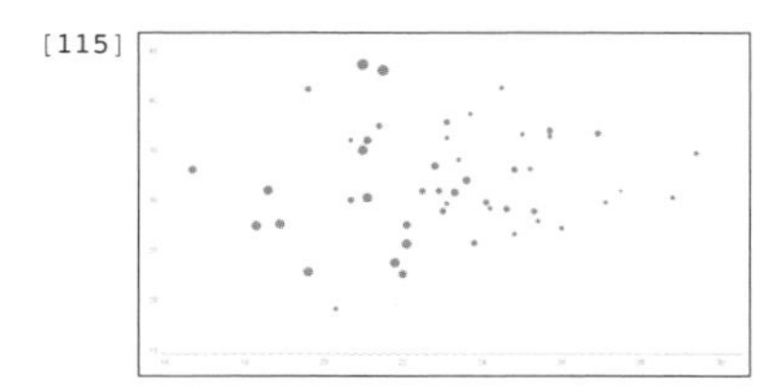

[116]

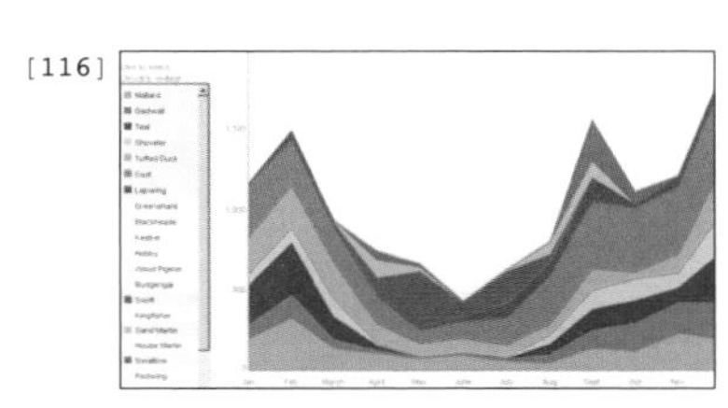

[117]

[118]

[119]

[120]

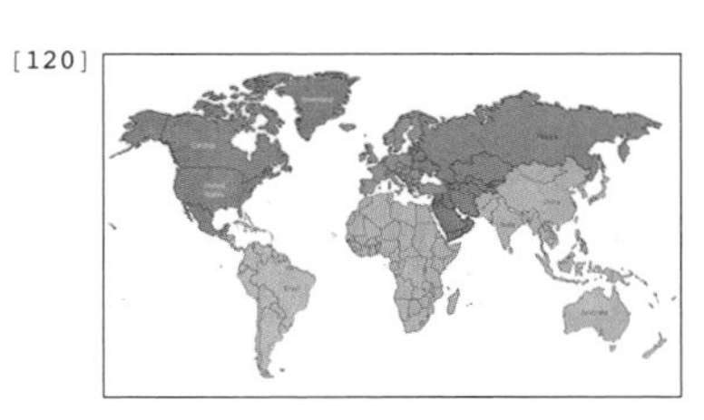

[114] Many Eyes, pie chart, IBM Research, 2008 [115] Many Eyes, scatter plot, IBM Research, 2008 [116] Many Eyes, stack graph, IBM Research, 2008 [117] Many Eyes, tag cloud, IBM Research, 2008 [118] Many Eyes, tree map, IBM Research, 2008 [119] Many Eyes, word tree, IBM Research, 2008 [120] Many Eyes, world map, IBM Research, 2008

For us as researchers, an important question is how people are using the site. To give you an example, two days after we launched Many Eyes, a user named Crossway uploaded a data set of name occurrences in the Bible. [121] For each verse of the Bible, whenever two names showed up in the same verse, there was a data point. He then created a social network of that data—a social network of the New Testament. He blogged about it and very quickly got hundreds of comments back. In fact, it became such a buzz that this visualization made its way out of the Catholic or Christian blogosphere into technology blogs. It was on BoingBoing, for instance, and there was a video on YouTube of someone playing with the visualization and commenting on what they were learning as they were playing with it. To come full circle, other people decided to upload their own data sets about the Bible onto Many Eyes, created visualizations, and blogged about them. So this was really a textbook example of a community that we didn't even know existed, who had tons of data, had a subject they were really interested in, and found an outlet that enabled them to visualize and talk about some of the statistics they were interested in.

[121] Many Eyes network diagram of name occurrences in the Bible, IBM Research, 2008

[121]

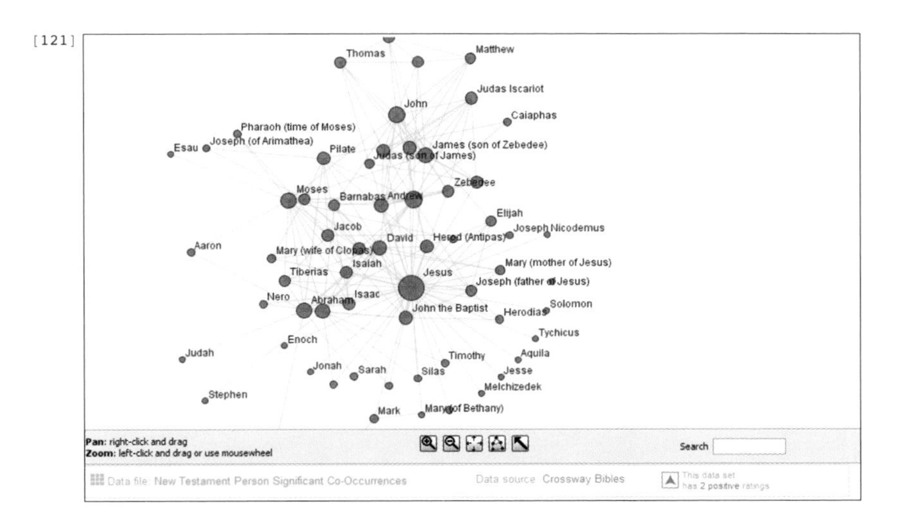

Thomas
Matthew
Judas Iscariot
John
Caiaphas
Pharaoh (time of Moses)
Esau
Joseph (of Arimathea)
Pilate
James (son of Zebedee)
Judas (son of James)
Zebedee
Moses
Barnabas
Andrew
Elijah
Jacob
Joseph
Nicodemus
Aaron
David
Herod (Antipas)
Mary (wife of Clopas)
Isaiah
Mary (mother of Jesus)
Tiberias
Jesus
Joseph (father of Jesus)
Nero
Abraham
Isaac
John the Baptist
Herodias
Solomon
Tychicus
Enoch
Judah
Timothy
Aquila
Jonah
Sarah
Silas
Jesse
Melchizedek
Stephen
Mark
Mary (of Bethany)
Pan: right-click and drag
Zoom: left-click and drag or use mousewheel
Search
Data file: New Testament Person Significant Co-Occurrences
Data source: Crossway Bibles
This data set has 2 positive ratings

Politics is huge on Many Eyes, as you can imagine, especially now during the election year. Political bloggers love the text visualizations. Besides the word trees, we also have tag clouds on Many Eyes for visualizing text. A lot of people will bring political literature to the site, illustrate it as tag clouds or word trees, and take the graphics back to their blogs, as for example this visualization of President Bush's State of the Union address in 2007. [122]

Recently, we've started to see institutions come to Many Eyes. This picture [123] comes from the Sunlight Foundation, an organization in Washington whose mission is transparency for government data. When they found out about Many Eyes, they created a whole set of visualizations about earmarks, took them back to their site, and started to talk about them. The blogosphere picked it up and ran with it, and the visualizations of the earmarks were shown in a lot of different places. They even ended up in the latest Lawrence Lessig Lecture on corruption [124], giving you a sense of how viral these visualizations can be, and how they can spark conversations and debates.

[122] Two-word tag cloud of President Bush's State of the Union address in 2007, by Many Eyes user. [123] Many Eyes visualizations on the Sunlight Foundation website [124] Many Eyes visualization featured in Lawrence Lessig's lecture about corruption in the government

[122]

Visualizations : president bush's state of the union address 2007

[123]

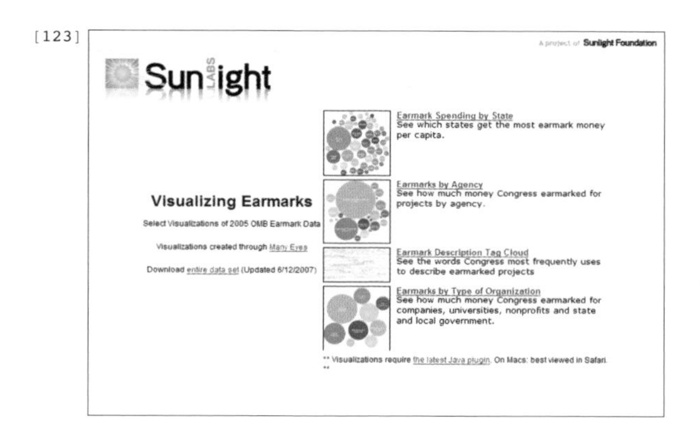

[124]

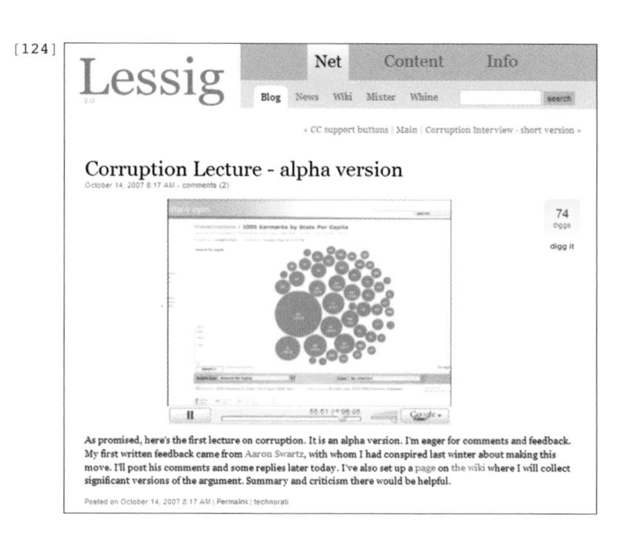

Many Eyes is completely public. Everything you do on the site—any data set, any visualization—is public and we state this very clearly, asking people not to upload any confidential data. But surprisingly, we get personal data all the time. People want to share this sort of information. These are just a few examples: The tag cloud is a visualization of John's freezer contents, but only the meat. [125] One user made a bubble chart of how she spent her afternoon on April 29. [126] She actually counted the minutes for everything she was doing that afternoon. And this bubble chart [127] was created by a kid who decided to look at all the socks in his family, categorizing them by whether they were his own or his Mom's, his Dad's, or his sister's. We've had people uploading their weight, their running logs, swimming logs, their writings, their Facebook friends [128], you name it. They are almost creating a mirror of themselves online.

The one thing that I'd like to leave you with is the idea that while these visualizations have an academic and scientific pedigree, we can start to think about them as a medium if we change our minds and our approach to them. When we think about visualizations as a way to communicate, it really changes the design implications and the possibilities of bars, charts, and diagrams. Thank you.

Applause

[125] Visualization of "John's Freezer Contents (only the meat)," by a Many Eyes user [126] Visualization of "How I Spent My Afternoon" by Many Eyes user [127] Visualization of family socks by Many Eyes user [128] Visualization of two Many Eyes users' social networks

[125]

[126]

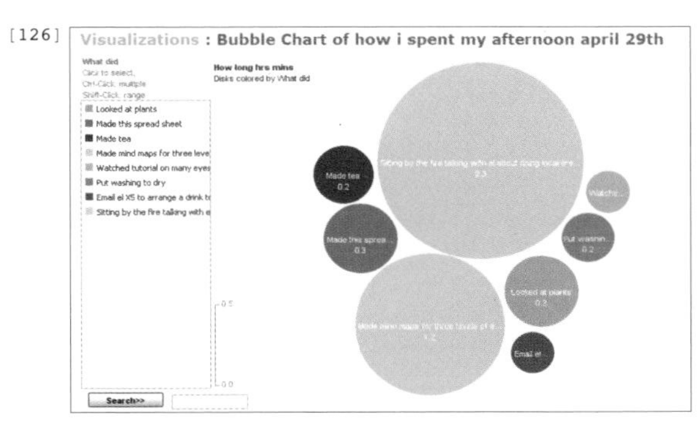

[127]

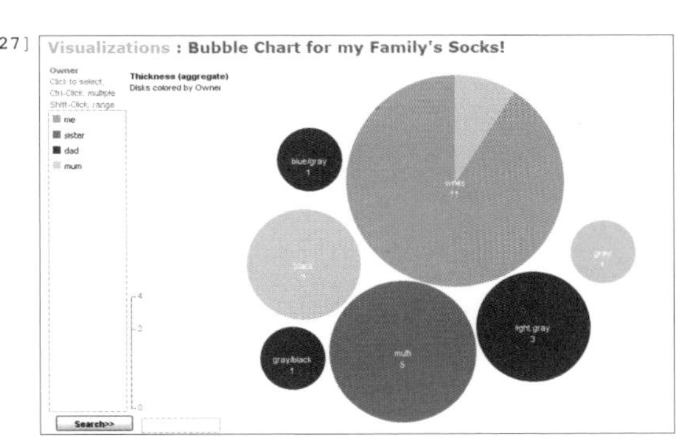

[128]

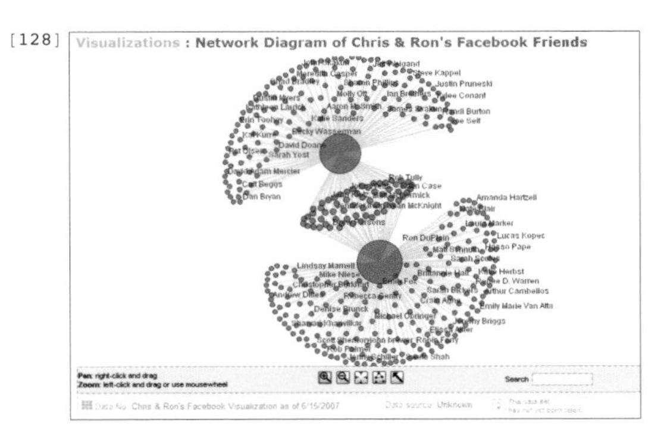

Enter all participants

. . .

Panel discussion

MAEDA: Thank you. That was pretty fresh, wasn't it? A little bit of business, a little bit of art, and a little bit of science—it's like going to Whole Foods.

Being the moderator I will now moderate, and I have a few questions for the people here to freshly address. I couldn't help but wonder, when I was seeing Many Eyes, whether this is going to put Steve's division out of business. Fernanda?

VIÉGAS: No, I sure hope not. We love the *New York Times* graphics, because they're so at the forefront of InfoViz. We're constantly waiting to see what they're going to come up with next. I also think there's a difference between what happens in Steve's department and what we're doing with Many Eyes. The graphic editors at the *New York Times* will spend a lot of time on every single data set, figuring out how to best represent it; a lot of thought goes into how to guide readers through a specific graphic and into the design decisions they make. Not to mention that this is all being done by experts, while on Many Eyes, the idea is to bring these tools to just about anyone and to see what they will do with it. We're starting to see, for instance, entire classrooms of kids playing with the site, and for the first time trying to understand what a data set is. So I think it's a very different way of dealing with data.

MAEDA: Steve, what do you think? Is she right?

DUENES: Yes. I think the difference between Many Eyes and the *Times* is similar to the difference between Wikipedia and the *Times*; one is a market place where people are exploring and exchanging data, while the other is a journalistic enterprise, where professional journalists are trying to tell stories. We're going out, we're reporting information, editing that information, and trying to develop graphic forms that tell those specific stories. So there's a little bit of a difference.

MAEDA: I have another question for Fernanda. Fernanda, will Many Eyes put Andrew Kuo out of business? What do you think, Andrew?

Laughter

KUO: Yes and no. I think the more you make these things, the more you're concerned with concepts and ideas. Anyone can make a cool-looking chart in a day. But if you can make something clever—if you can tell a real story—I think it's worth telling it again and again.

MAEDA: Steve, I have this vision of you firing up one graphic after another in this big pizza oven, but you mentioned to me in an earlier conversation that sometimes you have to lobby for that graphic—the one graphic that people don't get. Can you talk about that?

Laughter

DUENES: Well, sometimes we have to convince editors in the newsroom that they should publish some of the figures that we come up with.

MAEDA: Do you give them candy or cookies, or what do you do?

Laughter

DUENES: To give you an example, we had to push for a series of maps that we were playing with to cover the results of the 2004 presidential election. Editors often tend to be a bit conservative when it comes to charts, and they're not so comfortable when they see something new. In this case, we wanted to try something new, we wanted to get away from the idea of just coloring the geography, of just shading a county red or blue. Because the conventional shaded map really gives you the wrong visual impression. There are a lot of counties that are geographically large but don't have very many votes. If they are shaded one color, you get a visual impression that reflects the geography, not the actual vote. So we put together five maps that we wanted to show on one page. [129] On the largest map, we put circles, which were scaled according to the margin of victory, on top of each county, so what you end up with is a chart projected onto a map. That way, the geography doesn't determine how you scale the chart, it is just a base that the chart sits on. Another map on the page was a cartogram that distorts the geography so that each state takes the shape of the number of electoral votes it has. Because these maps were so unconventional, we had

[129]

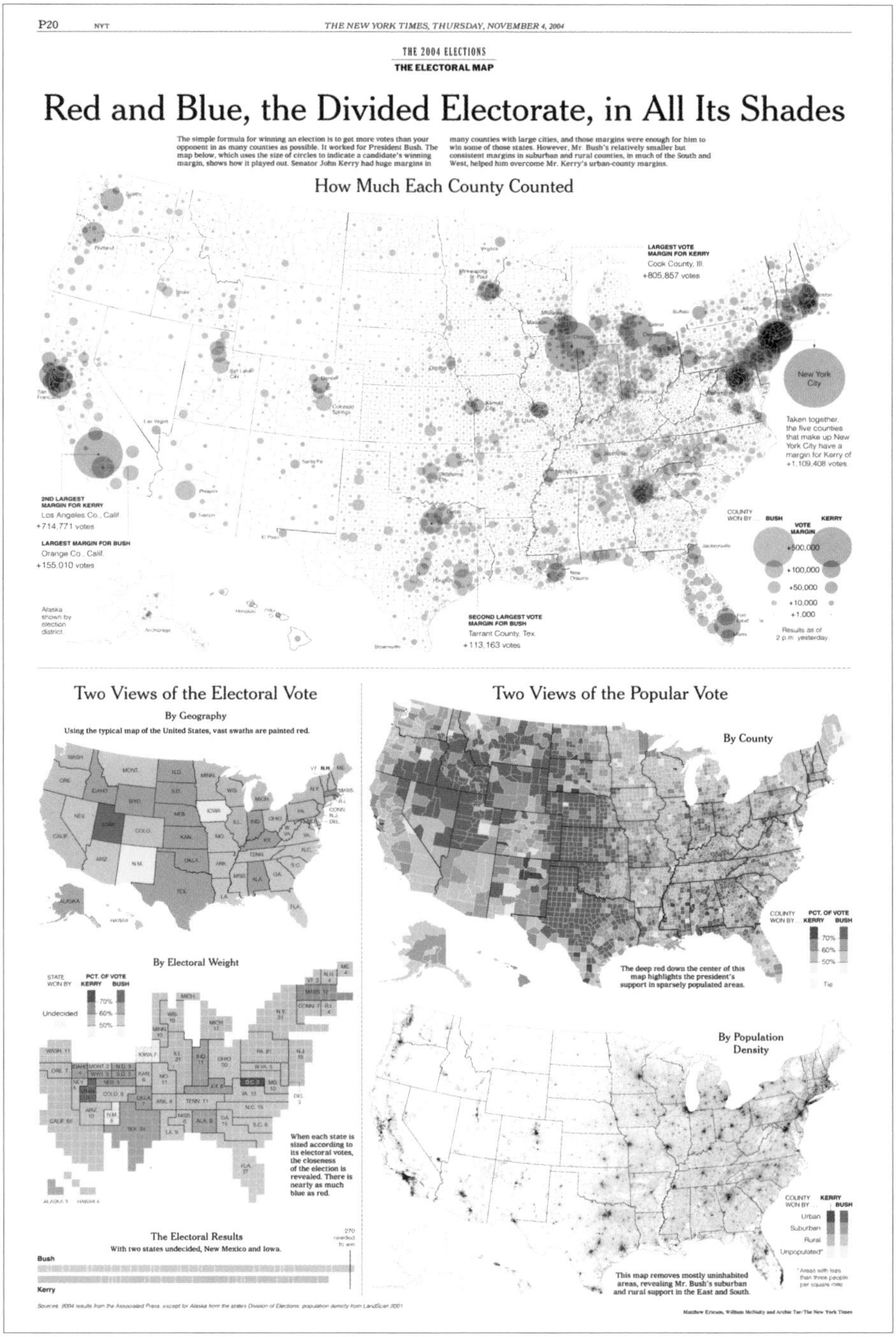

P20 NYT THE NEW YORK TIMES, THURSDAY, NOVEMBER 4, 2004

THE 2004 ELECTIONS

THE ELECTORAL MAP

Red and Blue, the Divided Electorate, in All Its Shades

The simple formula for winning an election is to get more votes than your opponent in as many counties as possible. It worked for President Bush. The map below, which uses the size of circles to indicate a candidate's winning margin, shows how it played out. Senator John Kerry had huge margins in many counties with large cities, and those margins were enough for him to win some of those states. However, Mr. Bush's relatively smaller but consistent margins in suburban and rural counties, in much of the South and West, helped him overcome Mr. Kerry's urban-county margins.

How Much Each County Counted

LARGEST VOTE MARGIN FOR KERRY
Cook County, Ill.
+805,857 votes

New York City

Taken together, the five counties that make up New York City have a margin for Kerry of +1,109,408 votes.

2ND LARGEST MARGIN FOR KERRY
Los Angeles Co., Calif.
+714,771 votes

LARGEST MARGIN FOR BUSH
Orange Co., Calif.
+155,010 votes

COUNTY WON BY ... BUSH KERRY
VOTE MARGIN
+500,000
+100,000
+50,000
+10,000
+1,000

Results as of 2 p.m. yesterday.

Alaska shown by election district.

SECOND LARGEST VOTE MARGIN FOR BUSH
Tarrant County, Tex.
+113,163 votes

Two Views of the Electoral Vote

By Geography

Using the typical map of the United States, vast swaths are painted red.

By Electoral Weight

STATE WON BY PCT. OF VOTE KERRY BUSH
Undecided
70%
60%
50%

When each state is sized according to its electoral votes, the closeness of the election is revealed. There is nearly as much blue as red.

The Electoral Results

With two states undecided, New Mexico and Iowa.

270 needed to win

Bush

Kerry

Two Views of the Popular Vote

By County

COUNTY WON BY ... PCT. OF VOTE KERRY BUSH
70%
60%
50%
Tie

The deep red down the center of this map highlights the president's support in sparsely populated areas.

By Population Density

COUNTY WON BY ... KERRY BUSH
Urban
Suburban
Rural
Unpopulated*

*Areas with less than three people per square mile

This map removes mostly uninhabited areas, revealing Mr. Bush's suburban and rural support in the East and South.

Sources: 2004 results from the Associated Press, except for Alaska from the state's Division of Elections; population density from LandScan 2001

Matthew Ericson, William McNulty and Archie Tse/The New York Times

[129] "Election Results, 2004," *New York Times*, 2004, design: Matthew Ericson, Archie Tse, William McNulty

to go to the politics editor and to the national editor and ultimately to the executive editor to finally get the approval to publish them.

MAEDA: Andrew, you seem to get away with a lot of stuff.

Laughter

KUO: So much.

MAEDA: Do you have to lobby anyone?

KUO: Well, of course not for my own personal work; thankfully, I have people who support me to get weird. But concerning the things I do for the *Times*, it's shocking to me how much I get away with.

MAEDA: How do you do that?

KUO: I have no idea. They know I'll be doing something, then I'll give it to them, and they'll just correct my spelling, and that's it.

Laughter

MAEDA: And they pay you for it, too?

KUO: They actually give me money, man!

MAEDA: Steve, are there fashion trends in information graphics? This year, pink and red are in, or this year, bar charts are very much in fashion?

DUENES: It does happen. Sometimes someone in the department will do something that sweeps through the department, and we suddenly find that we're charting everything the same way. For a while, we got a little too enthusiastic about circles, for example. There were times when we used circles when we should have used bars. Eventually, we got back in the right groove, though.

Laughter

MAEDA: So what's in this year?

Laughs

DUENES: Oh, I don't know what's in this year.

MAEDA: Fernanda, you're a doctor, and you're doing research. Are you a scientist?

VIÉGAS: I don't think about myself as a scientist, no.

MAEDA: I'm asking because I met Fernanda a long time ago, when she came to the MIT Media Lab for an interview. She was a young girl from Kansas—from Rio and Kansas—and she had so much energy and so much positive feeling. She wanted to do something involving computers in an aggressive way, and I said, "Well, you have to learn a program to do that." She said, "Okay, I will." And she went off and did it. Graphic design major turned super computer scientist—good for you, Fernanda. But a question for you: We've seen the many different visualization techniques you have on Many Eyes—the tree maps, the tag clouds, bar charts, and so on. Are these all that are out there, or is the Starship Enterprise looking for more planets to put in Many Eyes? To make Steve a little bit nervous.

Laughter

Laughs

VIÉGAS: I hope we don't make him nervous, but we're definitely looking for more techniques.

MAEDA: Do you ask people for the planets or do you come up with them yourselves?

VIÉGAS: We would like to open the site to the community and to enable people to contribute new visualization techniques to Many Eyes—that would be wonderful. But we're not there yet. I think most of the hurdles are legal rather than anything else.

MAEDA: Have you thought of paying people to do that? To have an open call for users to make Many Eyes fruits and vegetables?

VIÉGAS: That's a good idea, actually. We'll think about that.

MAEDA: Andrew, you went to RISD, but you're a fine arts student. I've seen it happen at RISD that people are uncomfortable with the fact that RISD is a design school rather than a fine arts school. Can you talk about that?

KUO: I think that kind of thinking really exists. Some artists are embarrassed to admit they went to design school; I myself had to get over that. I thought that way for years, because I felt there was this issue of credibility. But I sometimes think design is more of a worthwhile thing than art, because as a designer you're helping people. With art, you're just helping yourself. I fully believe in that, and I'll stand behind it.

Laughs

Laughter

Laughter

MAEDA: So in Andrew Kuo world, what color is art, what color is design?

Laughs

KUO: Dark brown, both. I'm kidding.

Laughter

MAEDA: Steve, the way you talk about visualization makes me feel safe.

DUENES: Good.

MAEDA: When you're talking about a graph, it feels like a Mercedes-Benz kind of a diagram. I can really feel the quality. But you began your presentation with pie charts, so what makes a good pie chart?

Laughter

Applause

DUENES: Basically, you don't want too many wedges. Things get crazy when you have too many wedges. You also don't want only one wedge. That's it, those are the only rules.

Laughter

MAEDA: Be careful of the mono-wedge! Fernanda, is Many Eyes a science project?

VIÉGAS: No, I think about it much more as a design project than a science project.

MAEDA: That's interesting. I've noticed that most scientists are not allowed to be happy and funny. I'll never forget how I was trying to sell the idea of a math film festival at the MIT math department. My math professor got me in a room with all the math professors, because he wanted me to sell this idea to his colleagues. My math professor was actually the one guy who was normal and funny, but all of the others weren't very funny. They asked, "Why would anyone come to a math film festival?" I said, "Well, you're mathematicians. You guys are cool, you guys are pure." And they all looked even more depressed and said, "Pure? Do you mean boring?"

Laughter

In Many Eyes, I think you're emphasizing the humor of graphics, and that's important to you, isn't it?

VIÉGAS: Oh, yes. I think that making things playful is very important. We see that in the way users are relating to the site.

MAEDA: Have you clustered diagrams in terms of humor, sadness, or fear?

VIÉGAS: No, but people have actually created diagrams of what colors relate to what sentiments the most. For instance, someone created a network diagram of emotional responses to color; whereas red seems to be related to love, anger, and aggression, black is related to power, fear, and confusion.

MAEDA: Andrew, what about you? How important is humor in your charts?

KUO: Humor is important to my life, and I've found that it is helpful in my art but not a necessity. It's not a crutch.

MAEDA: Now just a general question here. In 1989, a good friend of mine told me about this fake Chinese proverb, which says that a picture's worth a thousand words, but it takes words to say that. Reactions, please.

Laughter

VIEGAS: For a project like Many Eyes, the interaction between images and words is at the very heart of what we're trying to achieve. Part of the point we're trying to make is that data analysis tools alone—such as visualizations—are not enough. You really need to be able to communicate around these images and tools in order to make sense. You need both words and pictures.

MAEDA: Steve, in your presentation you brought up the program Adobe Dimensions. Can you talk about that a bit? It's gone now, right?

DUENES: We actually still use it on some occasions. My friend and colleague Archie Tse mastered Adobe Dimensions, and now he won't give it up. It's actually a perfect application for extruding basic shapes. It's a 3-D rendering program for people who are very, very slow and who couldn't make the leap to Maya or Strata software. Adobe Dimensions is just vector-based. It's very simple. You can revolve things, you can extrude things.

Laughter

MAEDA: It's sometimes wrong; that's why it was discontinued, isn't it? The graphic comes out wrong?

DUENES: Yes, but you know, you just try it again and again, and eventually it's right.

MAEDA: While you guys were talking earlier, I couldn't help but wonder about this next question. You are all working in the digital medium, and I'll never forget the year when *National Geographic* "moved" the pyramid by digitally manipulating photographs. So what is a digitally manipulated digital diagram?

Laughter

DUENES: I think this is a serious question. Part of what I was talking about earlier is that we don't want to suggest that we know more than we do. If you extend a graphic beyond your knowledge, I'd consider it a manipulated diagram.

MAEDA: Fernanda, I love the thumbnail function in Many Eyes, which enables you to take a diagram and say, "I want to talk about this diagram." Whose idea was that?

VIÉGAS: We knew from the beginning that we had to have a way of pointing at things. That was clear to all of us. We wanted to create a site that was completely asynchronous, so that even when I'm not there you can still make sense of what I'm trying to say.

MAEDA: How many people did it take to make Many Eyes? Are you allowed to say that?

VIÉGAS: Yes. Our team is very small, only four people.

MAEDA: Ooh, hard work. Are they RISD grads?

Laughter

VIÉGAS: No, unfortunately not.

Laughter

MAEDA: I couldn't help but notice that all of you use rollover graphics. My good friend Chakako Chernama, who runs the Tokyo Type Director's Club, always says that she can't stand interactive graphics, because it's like being a dog sniffing for a bone on the screen. How do you react to that?

Laughter

DUENES: I think a dog sniffing for a bone isn't necessarily a bad thing.

KUO: That's what I thought, too.

DUENES: Sniffing for a bone is the same thing as looking for a reward. Hopefully, the navigation of a graphic is designed so it's clear where to find the reward, which is the information revealed on rollover.

MAEDA: Fernanda, before this panel session, you spoke passionately about scatter plots. Why are you so fascinated by scatter plots?

VIÉGAS: I'm actually not fascinated by scatter plots, but what was interesting to me was what Matt Ericson, who works with Steve at the *New York Times*, said at a conference for InfoViz a few months ago. He told us that the graphics department had decided not to run so many scatter plots any more, because they found out that the readers couldn't understand them. That really surprised me, because a scatter plot is the easiest, most direct way to show correlation between two variables. So one of the things that illustrates is how easily you can fall into the trap of thinking that something is a very simple visualization technique, which everybody will understand, when that may not necessarily be true. People are very good at reading maps, they're very good at reading time-related graphics that run on an X-axis, but it's wrong to assume they will understand any graph that looks easy to someone who grew up doing graphs and charts.

DUENES: We do still run scatter plots, by the way. It's true that we were told that some of the figures we produce are overly complex and readers experience some difficulty understanding them, but if you look in the business section every day, you'll see the so-called Sector Snapshot, which is basically a scatter plot of different sectors of the economy.

Laughs

VIÉGAS: Good.

DUENES: This is one of the cases where we had to lobby to be able to continue to do visualizations like scatter plots.

MAEDA: Andrew, what's your favorite kind of plot?

KUO: I really use only about five different kinds of charts, so the bag of tricks is very small. But I like the circular diagrams I've been doing. By bending the X-axis, you can make something understood into something that is not understood anymore. Those make me happy visually. I think it's really important to be happy with what you make in life.

Laughter

MAEDA: Steve brought up the point of the honest diagram. I froze in my seat when you said that you chose the rapidograph style over some kind of super Google Earth type of rendering when you were mapping Saddam Hussein's hiding place. What about that? Are computers dishonest?

DUENES: They can be, if the operator is dishonest.

Laughter

MAEDA: There are probably dishonest people with pens, too.

DUENES: Yes, there are dishonest people with pens. There are a million ways to manipulate a set of statistics or data. You can visualize things in ways that distort the data. If you don't zero-base a line chart, for example, the change may look like more than it actually is. But for us in the graphics department it's just a goal to think about the nature of the data we have in front of us and to work through enough iterations of a chart until we come up with what we feel is an honest visual impression.

MAEDA: I recall this moment after I had stopped using the computer and was drawing something in an ink-drawing class, when I made a mistake and reached for the undo key. It was like a phantom reflex. Do you think that when you draw something, it has to be honest, because there is no undo key?

Laughter

KUO: I feel that the work I had been making right before I started with the charts was actually undoing everything. At least, that's the psychology behind the paper cutouts I showed you earlier. So you *can* undo it.

MAEDA: In the world of Many Eyes, what is the equivalent of hand-drawn? Could you have a button that allows you to outsource to someone in Greece? Do you envision some kind of hand-drawn visualization technique?

VIÉGAS: Not yet, no. Everything is still very much template-based. One of the very small steps we're doing toward something more personalized is allowing users to choose their own color, which is

Laughter

actually a big risk. People will sometimes choose very odd color combinations that don't work very well. For instance, someone will use a very light yellow against a white background, so the graphic becomes almost illegible. Or users choose colors that vibrate garishly against each other. But the choice of color was still one of the things we definitely wanted people to have. If someone is trying to show political data sets using maps of the United States and congressional districts, the colors there, for example, the red and blue, are really important and you need to be able to choose them. So that's our first small step toward empowering the user.

MAEDA: Let's talk computer programs for a second. Does this panel believe that the computer programs you're using are as advanced as they'll ever be? Will there be a major advancement, like the jump to hyperspace? And if so, when's it going to happen?

KUO: The companies probably already have it. They're just not giving it to us.

Laughter

MAEDA: It's in the vault. Aliens came and they're waiting for it too. Do you feel limitations in the tools right now?

DUENES: In the graphics department, we don't feel so limited. Maybe we just don't understand the possibilities, but the programs we use seem sufficient for what we do.

MAEDA: Fernanda, do you feel limitation by computation or sofware? You're working for IBM, so I know you have to be careful about what you say.

Laughter

VIÉGAS: No, it's okay to talk. For Many Eyes we're actually not using software programs such as Adobe. We're using Java and Flash and other programming languages, and the limitations there are different kinds of limitations. Much of Many Eyes is done in Java, so most of the visualizations you saw today were written in Java. As soon as we launched the site, people were asking, "Why are you doing this in Java?" Even people from MIT said, "It works, it's beautiful, it works really fast on my computer, but I hate you. Why did you do it in Java? Why aren't you using Flash?"

So we're starting to move into Flash right now, because it's more available. But there are still a few visualization techniques that require a lot of math processing, for instance the social network diagrams, which are very hard to do in Flash. Java's much better for that. So we have to deal with these platform issues, because we're working on the Web.

MAEDA: All three of you are very successful people at what you're doing. What is your advice for people who are trying to develop a career, who want to become like you? What do they need? Besides depression or whatever. What kind of person would you hire, Steve?

Pause

Laughter

DUENES: Well, there are a lot of different kinds of people in the graphics department. There are cartographers, we have a statistician, and we have people who are illustrators. But what everyone has is a basic journalistic wherewithal. We're looking for people who are curious about the world, who want to go out, gather information, and look at that information and tell a story with it.

MAEDA: Andrew, imagine five people show up at your door. They want to work with you desperately. Which will you choose? The tall one, the short one?

KUO: I would choose the one that's dying to tell me they're dying.

MAEDA: How do you tell?

KUO: You can tell.

MAEDA: Fernanda, how about you?

VIÉGAS: I think it would be awesome to have science people who are very good at some specific craft, but who are also willing to cross boundaries and do interdisciplinary work. I myself learned a whole lot; I went from graphic design to a place like MIT where I had to learn how to program out of the blue, and that just makes you think about things in a very different way. So I think being an expert in some field, doing something really well, and then being willing to grow in different directions is key. We would love to have people like that.

MAEDA: Thank you. I think it's time now to make this evening even more interactive and open it up to the floor. So, questions anyone, raise your hand.

AUDIENCE MEMBER: *I have a question for Fernanda. On Many Eyes, is it possible to continuously update the data so that it reflects new developments?*

VIÉGAS: Right now, no. Right now you have to upload your data set and it stays there, it's static. But we're working on a version that will do exactly that, where you can just point to a URL, and the visualization will automatically update according to new information.

AUDIENCE MEMBER: *Another question for Fernanda. Is there any kind of Wikipedia element on Many Eyes? Can people work collectively on a data set?*

Laughs

VIÉGAS: We're working on that as well. Right now, only the person who brought the data set to the site can edit it, but we want to open it up so that people can do it collectively, because I think that's powerful.

AUDIENCE MEMBER: *A question for Steve. How much leeway do you have with the data you're reporting. Is the data handed to you or do you go out and get it yourselves?*

DUENES: I'd say we go and get 80 percent of the data that we're dealing with ourselves. The people in the department are journalists, so we expect them to try to find data, to find stories. Often when a reporter will give us a data set, it's incomplete, so we'll go and complete it, but most of the time we're getting the entire data set ourselves.

AUDIENCE MEMBER: *My question is for Fernanda and it refers partly to what Steve was talking about earlier, about the objective, neutral presentation of data. Fernanda, you were saying that people on your site might choose the wrong colors. Do you also see that people are choosing the wrong schematic? Are they using a bubble diagram, for example, when they should be using a pie chart or a word tree? And if they're doing that, are you seeing the public commentary looking at that and discussing what the right choice is for visualizing a certain kind of data set?*

VIÉGAS: Yes, we do see that. Sometimes a user will have a poor choice of a technique for the data set they are trying to show. What tends to happen then is that other people will come along and visualize the data set again in a different way, saying, "Hey, have you tried visualizing this as a line graph as opposed to a pie chart?" So you see people pointing to other techniques, to learn by example, I guess.

Another thing that I thought was interesting is that sometimes—not very often—people use techniques in the wrong way but to a really cool effect. The stack graph, for example, that I was showing you earlier is usually used to represent historical data, so often you have a time element at the bottom. One user put categorical data at the bottom instead, which you usually don't want to do, because it doesn't make any sense. But because he used only two categories, it actually did make sense. And that surprised us. We didn't think about this. If you have very few categories, this is one new way you can use the stack graph.

AUDIENCE MEMBER: *Steve, do you have any idea on how well your graphics work, in the sense of how well your readers understand them?*

DUENES: We're totally blind. We have no idea if people understand what we're doing. Actually, that is not quite true. While we don't do a lot of user testing, there's a lot of peer editing. There are about thirty people in the department, so editors are constantly looking over each other's shoulders, and you get a lot of

Laughter

feedback when you're creating a piece. There are also layers of editing in the newsroom. The graphic goes to the reporter, to the line editor, and to the copy editor. Copy editors and backfield editors, who work closely with the reporters, react to the piece as a reader would—they tell you whether or not they understand the graphic—so we feel that for most of our figures that feedback gives us a clear sense of whether or not a piece is working.

In the last couple of years we've been doing more interactive graphics for the Web, and some of those are pretty complicated, so we now feel the need to do more traditional user testing to see how people are interacting with these figures. But to date there hasn't been a lot of that.

AUDIENCE MEMBER: *I have a question for any of you. I work on the Web and a lot of the people I work with engage with information architecture, and I'm just curious if you guys have any thoughts on how information visualization will lead to new revolutions in how we approach the Web?*

KUO: Personally, I think it's important to not concern yourself with those things and just see information visualizations as standing by themselves. I think for what I do, and the discipline I have, it's important to not get bogged down in that line of thought.

DUENES: I think of it a little bit differently. I think of reporting as the source of every visualization. You have to go back further than the visualization. You have to start by collecting good data, interesting data, data that is relevant. You can't do anything without data, so if you're not a good reporter, if you can't find interesting data—and if you're not a good editor and you're not discriminating about the data you report—then you're sort of nowhere. So that to me is the source of all those other things.

Visualizations are interesting only because they reveal something about an interesting set of data, an interesting piece of information. But you have to start with data. You have to start with reporting and research. Every good chart springs from that.

VIÉGAS: I can't bring myself to think about "information design," "interaction design," and "information architecture" as separate disciplines anyway. To me, they all belong together. But you do touch on an interesting point about presentation. I don't think we're at a point yet where we know how to do good presentations with interactive information visualization on the Web. I think we're working toward that, but I think we're just scratching the surface. The thumbnail function on Many Eyes, for instance, is just a small step. What does it mean to really think about these moving things, these interactive graphics, as something that you could really inhabit, that you could really have a conversation around? I think we're still very much at the beginning of solving that question.

MAEDA: You're basically talking about intellectual ownership, too. This is mine. I did this first. And now you are all coming to me because I was the first. Or you're sharing, you're saying, "Let's not worry about that," the West Coast kind of way.

Laughs

AUDIENCE MEMBER: *A question for Andrew. Are your graphics based on real data? Do you take notes during shows?*

KUO: I do. I just have a piece of paper and a pen, but it's important to me that the data is real. If I didn't take notes, I'd forget what songs a band played.

AUDIENCE MEMBER: *This question is for Steve, and it goes back to the pie chart you showed at the beginning. What is your take on the nontraditional doughnut pie, which is now out and about? The reason I ask is because a few of my clients are a little skeptical about using the doughnut as opposed to the real traditional pie chart.*

DUENES: Where do I stand on the doughnut versus pie debate? I think both are fine. If you look at European newspapers, you'll see that they use the doughnut much more frequently than they use the traditional pie, so perhaps the pie is a more American form. And we're patriotic, so we stick with the pie. But either

Laughter

Laughter

way it's not a distortion, it's an accurate representation of the data, so there's no right or wrong.

MAEDA: One is fried and one is baked.

DUENES: Right.

AUDIENCE MEMBER: *So it's not a bad trend?*

DUENES: I don't know if it's a trend. I haven't seen the doughnut all over the place.

AUDIENCE MEMBER: *My question is for Fernanda. Have you ever considered privatizing a part of your business? I realize that a lot of Many Eyes is about data sharing, but in our business, where you have clients who value confidentiality, you might not want to share that information with the Web. Have you ever considered doing anything like that?*

VIÉGAS: That's actually the number one request we get. Companies are asking whether they can run Many Eyes behind their firewalls or whether they can buy it. IBM is working on that in parallel to Many Eyes. We're just a very small research group, so we ourselves cannot do that. And for us, having the public site is really the basis of our research. We want to understand what happens when you have it out in the open. But, as you can imagine, IBM is looking into offering a privatized version of Many Eyes.

AUDIENCE MEMBER: *I have one more question. I look at what you do as almost a resource that allows me to see how a set of data plots out when you graph it. Are there any copyright issues involved with taking that information and redesigning it in a different way?*

VIÉGAS: That's a good question. As long as you don't use them for something commercial, as long as you don't try to make money out of the Many Eyes charts, you can use them in any way.

You can take screen shots, modify them, change the color of something, or take out labels, that's totally fine. The only thing we ask is that if you use a Many Eyes visualization, you credit it somehow. If you just use the data set, on the other hand, and completely redesign its visualization, you're free to do whatever you want with it, because then it's not a Many Eyes visualization anymore. Part of the reason why we wanted to have a direct link between the visualization and its data set is to enable users to do that.

MAEDA: I'm so glad you brought this question up, because I think more and more artists and designers have been needing to engage deeply in a conversation on intellectual property and copyright. In the world of "open" thinking, we don't worry so much about intellectual property, so that simplifies things. And I have to add that Fernanda and Martin are wonderful sort of 1960s-style, save-the-world researchers. Probably no one cared about their project until they put it on the Web, and suddenly the whole world cared about it, the lawyers popped up out of the silos and business people appeared, so that's a different era. Now they all love it, which is good and bad.

AUDIENCE MEMBER: *Steve, do reporters in other departments sometimes turn to your department to help them understand a data set, never mind whether it will go into the paper?*

DUENES: Sometimes. The *Times* has a couple of resources for that. In the newsroom there's a computer-assisted reporting desk staffed with people who specialize in managing and analyzing data bases. But there are also editors in the graphics department who are pretty good data analysts, so we develop relationships with reporters over time. It's quite common that someone will just come by informally and say, "Hey, I sent you this spreadsheet, can you visualize it, because I'm interested in trying to find interesting patterns." So that does happen.

AUDIENCE MEMBER: *Do you ever influence the lead of a story? Do editors sometimes change their story after seeing your graphics?*

DUENES: Yes, that happens. Usually, reporters come to us before they've determined what the lead of their story's going to be. They're looking for a lead, they're looking for the point in a particular data set.

MAEDA: Do you see an increase in writers who want your services? Are they lined up outside your office, waiting to get diagrammed?

DUENES: Yes, there's been a little bit of an increase recently, both for our desk and for the other desks that do this sort of analysis.

AUDIENCE MEMBER: *I have a question for Steve. What's the background of the average professional in your department? Are they graphic designers? And what is the structure of the department, how do the diagrams happen?*

DUENES: As I mentioned before, there are a lot of different kinds of people in our department. There are people with B.A.s, people with advanced degrees, trained cartographers, illustrators, and people who came out of the master's program for journalism.

In terms of how we work together—how the department is structured—we assemble teams very quickly to respond to different news events. Depending on what it is that we want to pursue—depending on the kind of figure that we want to create—we'll assemble a small team of people based on their skills and interests. If we know we're going to need a map, we'll choose someone who's good at creating maps; if we know we're going to need a particular piece of information, someone whose strength is reporting is going to be a part of that team. The team then works together to create the chart or map.

AUDIENCE MEMBER: *Andrew, do you or have you collaborated with someone else on a diagram?*

KUO: No, I do not like to collaborate with people on my charts, because then I become just an information producer. It's really important for me to think of myself as an author. It's all I got, and it makes these things walk. As soon as someone asks, "Can you chart all my ex-boyfriends?"—which someone has asked me before—it loses all of its power.

Laughter

AUDIENCE MEMBER: *A question for the panel. How important are accuracy, precision, and communicating a story to you? How do you rank these three things?*

MAEDA: Andrew?

KUO: I'm not really concerned with accuracy. Of course, it's important to fall back on accurate data, but what interests me most is the storytelling.

Laughter

MAEDA: Fernanda?

VIÉGAS: There are two things for us on Many Eyes that are really important. One is to spark conversation and discussion. This sort of storytelling is the whole reason why Many Eyes exists in the first place. Having said that, the issue of accuracy becomes important from the moment you realize that this is a public site on which anyone can upload data, because you have no assurance that the data is accurate or true. In that way, it's similar to Wikipedia, so having mechanisms that allow other users to check on the data is really important. From the beginning we made sure to have a direct link to the data sets, so anyone can check whether the data is accurate.

MAEDA: Steve?

DUENES: Accuracy is the most important thing for us.

MAEDA: It's the *New York Times*.

DUENES: Yes. If I don't say that, I'll be fired immediately.

Laughter

MAEDA: Before we end this evening, I want to add my own point. What I realize more and more is that artists and designers—creative people—are very good at dealing with ambiguity. And I just want to say that this unique skill to look at the world in weird, weird ways is needed more than ever today, because our world is very complex; it's very depressing as well. We need people who can figure out the world, and so I invite all of you here tonight to use this skill—to go out and show how creative people can lead the world. Go after it. Thank you very much, everyone.

Laughter

Applause

www.nytimes.com

www.andrewkuo.com

www.manyeyes.com

— ~~Plan~~ meanwhile ~~road~~ road repair
water treatm +
sorted trash

But these are not sexy problems with tech solutions

like private medicine — can deliver better care
for common problems but not uncommon